WHAT THEY'RE SAYING ABOUT
Spiriting around

"It's never too soon or too late to think about who you are,
who you want to be and what you should do about it, if anything.
In simple, practical language this book will help you do the
thinking, if you choose to."

—**Mario Cuomo,** *former Governor of New York State*

Spiriting around

A MODERN GUIDE
TO FINDING YOURSELF

Spiriting around

A MODERN GUIDE TO FINDING YOURSELF

MARTIN "MARK" TOMBACK

Mooring Field Books, Inc.
Cooper City, Florida

Spiriting around
A MODERN GUIDE TO FINDING YOURSELF
BY MARTIN "MARK" TOMBACK

Published by:

MOORING FIELD BOOKS™

Mooring Field Books, Inc.
9369 Sheridan Street, #555
Cooper City, FL 33024
Phone (954) 435-1672   Fax (954) 435-8662
mooringfieldbooks@msn.com
www.spiritingaround.com

First Printing 2006

Edited by Robin Quinn
Cover & Interior Design by Peri Poloni, Knockout Design,
www.knockoutbooks.com

Printed in the United States of America

Publisher's Cataloging-in-Publication
(Provided by Quality Books, Inc.)

Tomback, Martin.
    Spiriting around : a modern guide to finding yourself /
by Martin "Mark" Tomback.
    p. cm.
    LCCN 2004107510
    ISBN 0-9755248-0-1 (ISBN 13: 978-0-9755248-0-0)

    1. Spiritual life. 2. Self-actualization
(Psychology)—Religious aspects. 3. Success—Religious aspects.   I. Title.

BL624.T652 2006   204'.4
                                        QBI05-600063

This Book is Dedicated To....

My mother, Muriel Tomback (1919-2002):
No one ever loved me as much as you did.

My cousin, Hortense "Cousin Horty" Shweitzer (1918-2004):
She was my mother's cousin and her best friend for over
eighty years. And she was my friend too.

My wife, Shelley:
I love you for who you are.

My daughter, Joslyn:
You give me so many opportunities to love you.

My dog, Petey:
Welcome to the family.

My friend, Tom Grimm:
For being a person who does what other people talk about.
And by his example
Guides me to doing the right thing too.

I REMEMBER THE BLACK WHARVES AND THE SLIPS,
AND THE SEA-TIDES TOSSING FREE;
AND SPANISH SAILORS WITH BEARDED LIPS,
AND BEAUTY AND MYSTERY OF THE SHIPS,
AND THE MAGIC OF THE SEA.
AND THE VOICE OF THAT WAYWARD SONG
IS SINGING AND SAYING STILL:
"A BOY'S WILL IS THE WIND'S WILL,
AND THE THOUGHTS OF YOUTH ARE
LONG, LONG THOUGHTS."

Henry Wadsworth Longfellow

Acknowledgements

My first thanks goes to the technological revolution that allows one person to produce so much. Thanks for designing the computers and developing the software. Thanks for the internet, email, faxes, laser printers, and word processing.

Next, thanks to the Publishers Marketing Association and the entire community of self-publishing professionals who provide the core expertise needed to create high quality books. The cumulative knowledge they share through their writings and seminars has given me the foundation I needed to bring this book to life. Their contribution has been indispensable to *Spiriting Around.*

And thanks to the individuals who have contributed to making this dream come true; thanks to attorney Lloyd Jassin for his professional direction, thanks to editor Robin Quinn for providing the modern structure that released the ideas in *Spiriting Around,* and thanks to Peri Poloni for her wonderfully exciting cover design.

And special thanks to my wife Shelley and daughter Joslyn for respecting the time I needed to produce this work.

About the Author

I'm the same as you. I had the same experiences you had, the same goals, and the same problems. I'm a Jewish kid from Long Island, born in 1950 in Brooklyn, New York of loving parents who came from Brooklyn too.

But life prepared me in a strange way to write this book. I was exposed to a full range of human nature. I've been intimate with life's ups and downs. From two-dollar bags of dope in seedy New York apartments to champagne and caviar at UN embassy receptions, I've shared a lot. From no-matter hippies to community active Rotarians, I've known them both. I grew up in the sixties, a powerful time of change in this world. For human consciousness, it was a time of great social storms when love became dynamic in the world. These were storms of civil liberties whose time had come. Civil rights, women's rights, working rights, sexual rights, gay rights, spiritual rights, experiential rights, and the rights of citizens to demand from their government compassion and common sense all emerged as the cultural generations clashed in a shock of new ideas all happening at once.

I skipped a grade and won a National Merit Scholarship but barely got out of high school. A dynamic planet was too much for me to handle at the time. I was smart and had opportunities but my potential got short-circuited when I was caught up in the drug epidemic prevalent then. It made my youthful confusion that much harder and, in my case, came close to mental illness. And it was all very confusing because contemporary culture was sending out contradictory values everywhere. Right and wrong seemed whatever was convenient whenever somebody wanted something. And everyone had a different opinion. So what was right? What was true?

To complicate things more I was afraid a lot as a young man. Like most boys I was distracted by women but terrified how to act around them and communicate my feelings. And I wanted a taste of the huge feast I saw spread before me on TV. But I couldn't figure out how to get it. So I decided to rebuild myself.

My awakening was in the early seventies when I started reading the Edgar Cayce books. I began experiencing conscious moments of reality. Later I was drawn to the New Age Movement and its odd mysteries, benefiting greatly from the many approaches others had found for examining consciousness. And I healed myself. Through books, seminars, endless contemplation, affirmations, more affirmations, positive thinking, and self-love, I retrained my mind. That meant examining my emotions, evaluating my thoughts, and changing the habits of a lifetime. It wasn't easy but what else could I do? What was more important? I wanted to be happy. And the future promised me self-confidence and an exciting world to use it in.

I wanted to write this book for a long time. I always felt I had something to say that would help others. But I had no idea of the high price the research would ask for. Who would embark on such a journey if they had to consciously live the cost before paying the price? All I knew was it was the right thing to do. Then I did it.

Contents

Introduction

So, how to be grown up? How could it be easier? How can growing up be less of a chore? Like anything else it takes steps. Your edge is the spiritual step. And it's not so much about believing in something you can't see as it is in trusting that spirit can work for you. Most people will do what works for them. But how are you supposed to know something you haven't experienced is worth your trust? And like sleeping in the backseat of a car while you drive through some city at night, it doesn't mean you've actually been there. A conscious presence is needed too. So you question whether or not God can really act on the things you want for yourself. Is God practical for you? So here are some answers. Here's a strategy to help you see how self-esteem and respect for God can define your success.

Spirituality isn't a foreign language. It's your natural voice. And it can be your everyday consciousness if you want it to be. It's not something that has to be learned like auto mechanics or cooking. It'll come to you easily if you let it. You just have to expect it. It's yours from the start and it's in everything you do. And it isn't limited to hushed tones, ecstatic jubilations, or reverent body language. You can walk life as a conscious spirit if you accept yourself as part of God. It's always there whether you know it or not. So why not know it and use it to make your life better.

This book takes on life face to face because spirit is not an esoteric exercise. It's the tool you use to manage your life. And like the old saying goes, "It's the right tool for the right job." Spirit's not separate from life. It's fully engaged in it. And understanding your spiritual side will make everything easier for you, from paying your electric bill to kissing your lover.

Spirit can lead you to the life you want. It takes some personal housekeeping though. It's not blind faith. It just asks you to see more than what your physical senses tell you. Like everything, spirituality's based on performance. It may be judged by God but it's evaluated by you. And it gets its value from your complete success, not the achievements that must be won over and over every day.

It's a functional understanding that spirit is a practical approach to life. And that it supports your desire to succeed. Spiritual consciousness gives you employable tactics to depend on to solve your daily problems. It's not an illusion of self-control that's reinforced by temporary successes. It's the practical face of spirituality that empowers your abilities because it focuses your Godly nature on your problems.

You can live your spirituality every day and be successful at it because you have help. You're a part of something greater than yourself. And you can be greater than life when you harmonize with God's support. So here's the help.

This book is about you qualifying your personal values. You can do it but you have choices to make. And it's your responsibility to ask if spiritual solutions can be practical answers to your questions. You can see it in a religious context or not. Either way, spirit's a part of it. It's why you're alive. You've got a lot to learn but you already know the answers. It just takes work to get to them. Life's challenges don't end. So we have to find ways to get along with each other as we move to its changing rhythms.

A good trick is to have a personal mission statement like big corporations do. Keep it simple, a brief guiding thought that embodies a core set of values you can trust even when you can't think straight. And it should be something that grows with you so it stays relevant to what you want.

Life resists us. So the purpose here isn't to tell you what to do but show you a way to think and release your sincerity. That's your connection to God. The simple reason for this book is people are suffering needlessly waiting for what they could learn here, ideas that could help them lead a happy life. People have different needs. Here are some answers for some of those people. I hope it helps as many as it can.

These are contemporary explanations for some of life's questions. The truth is 95% of life is just common sense. But you need values and you have to pay attention. You have to know how to get the information you need and find a way to trust it. And once you accept it you have to be able to empower your courage to do something about it. A big part of life is just uncomfortable, not really bad. So you, as a soul in nature, seek the relevance that connects your life's solutions to your responsibilities to the world around you.

It must be done and you'll do it. It can be easier though. That's this book's approach. Life's the obstacle, not God. God's the idea to use in everything you do to overcome that obstacle. And God accepts this responsibility wholeheartedly.

Life's demanding and we want quick solutions. That's reasonable and God knows it. So in asking for God's help you empower yourself and command the forces that serve God. This is about making God present in your conscious life. But God's performance must be dependable for you to trust it as part of your strategy. Your responsibility is to make a commitment to that trust and learn all you can about it. It won't take long to trust it because it works. God is love. So this book asks you to go beyond the comforting limits of religion and let that love be your philosophy. Your problems won't end but how you feel about yourself can give you the confidence to accept life for what it is. And let happiness be your way of life.

THIS IS YOUR BIRTHRIGHT...
TO CHALLENGE ADVERSITY
AND OVERCOME IT.

IT'S IMPOSSIBLE TO
BE DEFEATED.
LIFE'S NOT CREATED
LIKE THAT.

CHAPTER 1

Start Here

LiFE'S RESiSTANCE

You're not alone! What you're going through and should be expecting are the same challenges every human being has been called on to encounter and surmount. It's life's natural resistance. Its purpose is to make us stronger through the tribulations of our experience and prove to ourselves that we're infinitely greater than any difficulty. It's the way we grow as human beings. And it's how we add to these experiences that we build the foundation for our future. Your future, with civilization's, depends on these challenges as the nourishment that energizes creation as it presses against that resistance. And it's up to you to create the assets you use to do it.

There's a TV news clip from the Viet Nam War where a soldier is interviewed by a news correspondent during the Battle of Hue. With bullets flying the weary young soldier ducks for cover behind a stone

23

wall then turns to the camera and says that he should really be back at home in school. Next with simple eloquence he adds, "This really stinks!" Then taking a deep breath and focusing on what he must do the soldier rises to the top of the wall and resumes firing his weapon. Unfortunately a lot of what we do in life falls into this category. We just have to handle whatever comes up no matter how hard it is. So this book is to help you deal successfully with your experience and avoid any needless suffering.

My father, a World War II veteran, had a saying, "Things aren't so bad as long as nobody's shooting at you." We're all not graced with the wisdom of that experience but we can recognize wisdom when we find it. Whether it's from life, advice, or education, any knowledge that helps you live on this planet should be sought out, respected, and appreciated. You'll make your own decisions but you should have as much information as possible on where your decision might lead you.

Every day we see news from some battlefield where people are suffering from a war. They're not actors in some movie. They're really living those terrible conditions. But you have problems too. And your challenges while probably not that drastic are certainly more immediate. And they might be overwhelming you. They may seem hopeless and never-ending. They're sure to be difficult and frustrating. You probably think you don't have enough money or whatever it's going to take to solve them either. Of course this isn't true. They're just your challenges of the moment.

And it doesn't matter how long you've been dealing with them. In time you'll solve them. *They're all temporary.* They're lessons to be learned so you can create the foundation for your future knowledge. This is your birthright...to meet adversity and overcome it. It's impossible for you fail. Life's not created like that. You can only perceive it that way. Only your perception makes a defeat real for you. If you don't give up you can't lose. And a positive perception always gives you a new starting point.

We're all like test pilots—part scientist and part adventurer—someone who'd risk their life to explore an experience. Test pilots crave the extreme dimensions of life's possibilities. They don't look at death as defeat. They look at death as the potential price for living a full life. We should thank them for their gift. They serve as a model for living that prizes courage and exalts life. While we can't always choose such intense challenges, the way we meet life is the same.

Experience is the reward for courage. But they're lessons hard won. And the price we pay for our experiences can seem so expensive that we wonder if they're worth it. These experiences are definitely worth it, but people can certainly suffer them less.

FiNDiNG SOLUTiONS

While all problems are real so are *the solutions* to those problems. A problem has many parts but there's a core element to every difficulty. Once that's fixed the balance moves from unstable to favorable and you get a new starting point.

But sometimes we qualify solutions with limits that aren't really there. These are the rules of a solution, the characteristics we'll accept for defining its success. But you're the one who decides it. You decide its features and what's important. And there's always a choice of solutions available; each with its own advantages, requirements, and costs.

But you just can't do whatever you want. All solutions are governed by the laws in your community. They're the rules for cooperative living. And they're designed to have a prosperous environment for everyone who lives there.

Your solutions are substantially dependent on the resources you have for meeting your challenges. These include your financial resources, your money and getting good value for it, and your time which represents your dedication to working out a problem. Also important is your personal support, the friends and family who'll help you. And naturally, your solutions are limited by your physical, mental, and emotional abilities as well as your experience, knowledge, and maturity.

Within this framework are a number of factors you can use to your advantage. There are positive things to be embraced and negative things which should warn you to use caution. As an added challenge the factors you deal with and the resources you have are constantly changing. Sometimes they get better and sometimes they get worse. The best part is you can use *them all*. Even a bad situation has new opportunities.

Like it or not, things are the way they are. Whether you think it's fair or not doesn't change it. But your desire and effort can change it! And it's your responsibility to change it! You can be successful! It's your birthright.

SPiRiTiNG ᴀROUND EXERCiSE:

Learning from Your Past

Part I

Look at your past challenges but don't judge them. This is only to see how you did things before. How did you go about solving those problems? What were your resources? What were your priorities? What actions did you take? What helped the most? Who helped the most? What did you regret? How did you know the problem was solved? What did you learn? Knowing what you know now, what would you do differently?

Part II

Now choose a problem you're facing today. Which lessons from Part I can be used to solve it? What else might be holding you back? And how far can you push those limits without going past them?

THE ROᴀD HOME

To complicate things you'll find not all the facts you have are accurate. It's part of every problem and you just have to deal with it. It's annoying and frustrating but accepting it as part of the problem helps you develop your desire to pursue what's real.

And not everything unexpected is wrong. Life's an assortment of questions. And beliefs are different for everyone. What's right for someone else may not fit you *at all.* So you have to be open to learning what you can and apply an inquiring eye to everything you find. So ask questions. Ask for advice. Question the logic of everything. Ask yourself, "Does it make sense to you?" "How's it going to happen?" "Where's it going from here?" And keep questioning! Find opposing points of view and see the reasons behind them. Then decide for yourself. The truth will make sense to you. You'll feel it. Common sense and human nature don't change. Learn about it and accept it because people are forever faithful to it.

Your knowledge creates opportunities for you to make more combinations from your thoughts. So you'll see *more possibilities.* By exploring these alternatives you'll develop new perspectives for solving the problems in your life. This means more opportunities for you to create your happiness. The purpose in accumulating information is to prepare your mind with a broad base of possibilities that energize your ideas.

Situations can be as terrible as they are but your ability to change your perspective will always give you the flexibility to adjust to any circumstance. And you'll always have this ability as long as you can think, compare, and make choices. And your comfort will come from your plans to meet those circumstances.

Your direction's what's important, not the situation. By a simple intention hopelessness can be changed to hopefulness. That means there's no obstacle that can ever prevent you from having your dreams come true. From your beliefs and efforts your consciousness can develop a positive attitude. Positive means that no matter where you are you're always moving forward towards your goals.

So you should always be clarifying your goals. The details make your desires visible. It helps you become consciously aware of what you want. And it eliminates the waste and delay in seeking unnecessary distractions. The more you know about what you want, the clearer your path will be. You'll instinctively know where you are and where you should be. And you'll easily see what you have to do to get there.

CHOOSE TO BE SUCCESSFUL.

Success feels good so why avoid it? Why do we ever resist love and retreat from feeling good? How often have you challenged yourself at the instant you discovered you liked something? At the split second your heart opened up to some new possibility, you closed it down. And you failed the challenge. When you're afraid of confronting your fears you become conflicted, saddened, and ashamed. And your only comfort comes from denying the truth.

This doesn't mean to understate the difficulties you'll have in understanding yourself. It's a normal part of life and it always has been. But today you can lean on a mature global consciousness to help you. The world today includes the sophisticated skyscraper civilizations of modern cities as well as the forest cultures of the deep jungles. The lifestyles may be different but our lives are the same. And it's this expanded database of human nature that provides the impetus for modern social growth.

Your success is revealed by what excites you. Those conditions are a physical representation of your happiness. Without them it's impossible to be satisfied. And when something important is given away, regret arises and a sense of "being without" results. Only when the things you want are an active part of your life will you feel complete. So keep asking yourself, "What makes you feel really good?"

It's not so easy though after you've put so much energy into rationalizing the concessions you've made to life. So your first move is clear. You have to identify what's making you feel bad. You might resist confronting the answers but the question is simple. And you'll find comfort in your honest intentions because you already know the answers. It just takes courage to meet your uncomfortable feelings.

But when you accept them, you'll know what's real. And that's worth the battle.

Once you embrace your feelings you'll see which were twisted by doubtful thoughts or dependent on someone's opinion. You have to feel your feelings. You have to exercise them so they'll be strong to serve you like they should. False beliefs are too high a price to pay just to eliminate the chronic pain that comes with living in a social world.

You created your world and you can change it. Not the past or an unpredictable future can hold you back. The universe supports you. Clear goals guarantee your success. So, go for it!

On the way don't fall into the trap of worrying about what others might think of you. For those who love you, anything good for you will be right for them. And don't worry about your enemies either. They'll find a reason to hate you whatever happens. A good reason won't change their opinion about you one way or the other. The only ones who'll judge you are those confused about their own lives. And all they want is entertainment. They don't know you and don't care about you. They have no real values and excuse their oblivion with worthless comparisons.

You'll find that about 10% of the people you meet will like you for no particular reason. And you'll get along with them easily. Another 10% will dislike you for no particular reason. And there's nothing you can do to change their minds. 60% of people will tolerate you and you can get along with them if you want to. Then there's the other 20% who just don't care. You can have some kind of relationship with them. Just don't expect too much. Of course this is a joke. But there's some truth in it too. It's that you can be discriminating in your relationships when you know what to expect.

PATiENCE & PERSiSTENCE

Don't be discouraged how hard things can be. Building a life takes time. Everything does. Things that are important can take a very long time. It's not ours to judge how long it takes to make something right. But you can be sure that someday you'll look back on your life with pride in your accomplishments and satisfaction in the person you've become when you do want things done right.

It hurts though while you're working hard waiting for your life to change. It takes time and you want it to be done. You probably have no patience for any more of the suffering you've already had. You want to feel good now. You want to be in control. Just keep in mind that no problem is beyond your ability to overcome it and no problem lasts forever either. Healing takes time. But there's no better use for your time. What's more important? What's more precious than loving yourself?

You're doing that very thing right now. You're on the path you hope brings you what you want. And that path becomes clearer as you go. Here you'll meet the conflicts and problems that have always existed in you. Maybe you've suppressed those difficult parts or avoided them till now. Well shun them no more! Now you can embrace every part of your personality as an important piece that completes the puzzle of your happy world.

As you meet your challenges, whether you know it or not, parts of you are always working to create your happiness. There's no emotional confusion that can undermine the part of you that yearns to succeed. The biggest challenges aren't physical no matter how formidable they may appear. Nature's wonders are the perfect proof. If life says something has to live under water to exist then it'll live under water. And if life says you need something satisfied in order to be successful then that'll happen too.

You can always trust that no part of you is ever bad or wrong. Personal problems are needed for development. They create the resistance you need to grow. It's part of God's plan for the universe. You just need to see life from the right perspective for it to make sense. God's unfailing support is constant and everywhere. The purpose of any situation turns on that perspective. And it's from that point of view that you create your happiness.

STAy FOCUSED.

Being confused about your goals can be frustrating. But until you're clear on what you want you'll have to do the best you can with what you know. That's okay though. Having patience is part of the process. Just remember that everything's a temporary situation and there's nothing wrong with it.

But without goals to guide you your path forward is just a guess. Solutions are hard to clarify because a question without a goal is always, "What's the problem?" What you can turn to is your sense of ability—knowing that if you can figure out what's important, you can solve the riddle, and have your happiness

There's a part of you that's always asking questions of your whole self. You have the innate ability to want a better situation for yourself. You have the ability to choose. You have the ability to change anything you want to create the vision of what you want your life to be. So we constantly examine our situation. Your divine ability is you can adapt to any circumstance. In any situation at least you can change your perspective. When change occurs paths are created. Some are for seeing the future and others for taking a step.

The key is, "Don't defeat yourself!" This is your experience and you can make it what you want. You possess the inner knowledge that nothing can stop you. And that anything can be achieved over time. That's your birthright too. This is what you're trying to understand. It's not about a lifestyle, some convenience, or boastfulness. It's your bountiful nature. So use it.

A contradictory planet offers confusing guidance. So, mass consciousness can help you. It averages things out. It gives us our contemporary values. And it gives us a basic structure about things. But it's not everything. And it can't stop you from having what you want for yourself. That's up to you. There's no standing still though. You're either going forwards or backwards. But even your intent to do better is enough to move you ahead.

SPiRiTiNG ARoUND EXERCiSE:

Ask yourself what you want. But don't struggle with it. Enjoy it. And be real. Its only limits should be respect for yourself and fairness to others. When someone else's opinion shows up in your thoughts you should question its importance. And ask yourself if you're questioning your dreams out of love or fear.

NO LOSERS ALLOWED

So what happens when your time runs out and you haven't achieved your goals? Is your failure complete? Is your life a disgrace or is everyone's life a success no matter what they've achieved? Spiritual truth is that we all die well with the same love and dignity in God. Dignity in dying is the acceptance that our turn at life is complete.

And knowing that every life is a success should give you the underlying satisfaction that dignifies your daily purpose.

Your dignity, the belief that you're naturally successful, should be your comfort as you ride out life's storms and surmount its obstacles. You don't have to be a slave to interpreting the meaning of every event in your life. And you shouldn't define yourself by the circumstances you find at one point in your life. Your consciousness of the dignity God bestows on each of us is enough reason to be joyful. *Dignity is realizing that you're important and valuable, if only by your existence.*

That's your potential for greatness in life. Greatness...not just getting by or being a survivor but the success that satisfies your soul. It may not be apparent. Or you might think it's impossible. But somewhere inside you, you know it's true. It's in you, dormant maybe, but alive and healthy. And it's waiting for you. It is you. It's every human being's essence as it comes from God, the loving power that supports you.

Your happiness has a schedule with specific conditions it needs to express itself. So you must be patient because it can't be rushed. But you can prepare yourself while you wait and be watchful because many opportunities on their surface may seem insignificant. But like the Three Kings who waited for the one who'd bring a great light to this world, you can have the character of a king too.

Right circumstances vary and they're different for everyone. Sometimes they're obvious. Other times they'll make sense to just one person. It might be a new idea joined with good financial resources and the right personal attitude. Or it might be the right skills being at the right place at the proverbial right time. It can even be someone's determination in facing down a problem that only their commitment can overcome. And it could be the right group of people whose combined talents manifest the increased ability that helps them accomplish more than they ever could have done by themselves. Whatever it has to be, it will be. The solutions are infinite. It means that whatever circumstances you need to succeed will happen. The magic is that whatever the situation, each of us possesses the potential for opportunity.

Your challenge is to look for the right circumstances, have the patience to wait for them, and trust them when they come. So you should cultivate your life with skills and friendships that allow your energies to grow. This will help you define who you are now! And help you to become the person you want to be in the future.

IT'S YOUR WAY.

One by one you'll solve your problems. You can eat an elephant a bite at a time if you have to do. You have the ability. But it's *your choice*. And it's not a race or competition. You can take whatever time you need to maintain a comfortable momentum. This means achieving success completely. And completeness means there's a right way of doing things. And you decide what the specifics are. But first you have to define it to create it. Then you'll know it when you have it.

To start, just know that what's right is determined by you without you sacrificing your values. And getting by should never be enough. There's a right way to have something and that's the way it should be if you want to feel complete. It's your advantage to settle for nothing less. To have your happiness just the way you want it makes you stronger even if it takes longer. You have reasons for your requirements even if you're not conscious of them. And when something important to you is missing your future is adversely affected both emotionally and physically. You have to accept that you can be who you want to be...exactly, correctly, and completely.

You probably just want to speed through everything and be done with your problems. But you should be careful not to create new burdens in your rush to solve them. Believing that you'll eventually find a way to succeed should give you the comfort you need when success seems beyond your efforts. Remember, there's no schedule. And there's no one to compare yourself to as far as how well you're doing. There's no rightness or wrongness about how to feel good. And that's what you really want. So it's about making the decision to have what you want—and then having it.

HAVE DIGNITY

You have to see yourself as successful regardless of circumstances or anyone's opinion. Other people's points of view are still important though. There are people you trust who love you. And their advice is invaluable. But what success means to you is your responsibility. No one can feel your elation in success or the pain of your disappointments like you do. And even though divine, compassion's only a mirror. It's saying, "See. Love has not failed. Here it is in another." So it's ultimately up to you to solve life's riddle for yourself.

Loving relationships are sublime and comforting. And based on mutual respect they're moral. They're a benchmark for our opinion of ourselves. Respect for individual dignity is the measure of any relationship. And there's never a good reason to compromise it. For any problem you can always find the right compromise where love's present. But love can't express itself without dignity. It's this respect for self-worth that holds relationships together and guides them in business and romance.

DiGNiTy?

Dignity, what's that? It's an understanding of the extraordinary value you already have as a human being. There's nothing to earn or create. It already acknowledges your fair place in society. And even in social settings it recognizes that your first responsibility is to yourself. But how you dignify yourself is up to you. You create its character. So accept yourself. Your principles and beliefs are decided by you. Your dignity will respect whatever happiness you choose for yourself. The first step is to know it.

Social environments assault our dignity. People will try to categorize you to fit neatly into their way of living. It gives them a sense of security and balance. But you want to know more about life and how every environment affects you. Today it's more complicated because besides the kid next door, modern society makes the media our neighbor. And like everyone else they have their own agenda. So you have to sort it all out. And you'll need your dignity to do it right.

Dignity is at a crossroads for civilization. It's because there's so much information today. Just realize that it's you who control it. You decide what you'll watch, listen to, or read. And you decide its value. But don't worry. Communication is our natural connection and you were born an expert at it.

The messages we share have stayed the same for thousands of years because people haven't changed. They're the same questions we've always had about purpose and survival. And you'll find the answers in the dignity you have in being honest with yourself. It's just common sense. It's the same for everyone and it proves itself every time.

So what about the quiet terrors we suffer every day? You're not alone there and you'll never be alone. If there wasn't one other person who knew that you needed help, the universe would always support you as an inseparable part of itself.

SPIRITUAL SUPPORT

Opening your mind to your spiritual dimension can help you. Its eternally fresh perspectives, loving comforts, and fairness make new opportunities available to you. The spiritual world waits with a wealth of wisdom for you. And it gives it away freely as it shares in your successes.

To be spiritually blind though is to ignore spirit's powerful support. That can make things harder than they have to be because you can reach your goals too easily only to find that you've missed the journey and its blessing of experience. Or you can bottle yourself up, struggling too hard against wasted resistance, as you go around in circles without gaining the wisdom of your goals. And instead of the harmony and fulfillment you're entitled to, you may go unfulfilled. And you'll waste a lot of time and effort that could've been used to accomplish other things you want.

FAITH

Faith, it's said, is belief in things unseen. That it needs no proof. So for someone who needs evidence for their faith there's really nothing that could ever satisfy them. Realistically though people do want proof. They want to be sure they can trust it. So you'd think that there must be proof. And there is. Faith isn't blind. It just sees reality beyond the physical world. It's the confidence in your soul that no other way of existence is possible. It's from faith that we question God's being. And the answer resoundingly rings, "Yes, God is here!" So faith is the answer to everything. And you can feel its gentle power in your soul's intentions. There it comforts us as the open door to spirit that welcomes God's miracles.

In its quiet energy faith flows as it reveals everything for your examination. And given the chance these simple beliefs can become your practical faith. But still it must prove itself by being dependable. That every cloud does have a silver lining and a practical purpose understood through faith.

But don't expect faith to be an easy ride. It demonstrates God's presence by challenging your spirit. So, it often shows itself at the last minute when everything seems hopeless. When only God can save you, God sends in the cavalry with bugles blaring and horses' hooves pounding—crushing every threat in their path. It makes movies suspenseful and it makes life suspenseful too. Because overcoming hopeless challenges is the essence of faith.

Fortunately, testing you to your limits isn't always necessary. But it does prove that you're never alone. God and spirit are fully aware of your plights. And though they may see life differently than you do, they're ready to help you however they can. Their love for you is constant and they'll gladly show you how to make faith's comforting peace a part your life. And it can be very convincing once you accept faith as your heritage.

THE WORLD OF SPIRITS

Also consider the possibility of a spirit world inhabited by loving personalities. Think of it as a place where dedicated spiritual beings offer their comfort and support. They include instructors who can guide you on your earthly journey. And they ask nothing of you but your belief. Whether you choose to believe in spirit guides or not, their existence doesn't change. But you have a better chance of success when you're open to the possibilities. And you might just accept them when they show you results.

Whatever you believe in is justified by the four options you have. First, something's true and you believe that it's true. Next, something's true but you think that it's false. Then, the reverse, something's false but you believe that it's true. And then, something's false and you believe that it's false. Remember, your beliefs don't affect the facts. The truth will be what it is whether you like it or not, whether it's convenient for you or not, or whether you argue it or not. It doesn't depend in the slightest way on your opinion even when you've made important decisions based on your mistaken beliefs. So you have to compare the cost of a misunderstanding with the benefit of seeing things as they are. It's because you always want to put your resources to work for you in real situations. Spiritual guidance is like that. It's hard to trust because it's hard to touch.

There's a lot going on in the realm of spirit that relates to helping people on earth. There are different kinds of guides with their own unique gifts. And they all want to help you. But isn't arbitrary. There's planning and management. There's evaluation and oversight. There are some guiding spirits whose expertise is in practical matters while others are more helpful in understanding the aspects of a soul's growth moving through the infinite eternal universe. While they can all appreciate most things, some may have a limited perspective functioning outside their own domain. They excel at what they do best. A spirit guide may wisely leave matters to another spirit who's better able to help you in a particular area. Like life, spirit is a practical place. It means that when you understand how spirit works it can help you make better decisions. And it'll be easier for you to access your guidance. Above all, life exists for opportunities. It's the reason for creation. And you're not out there alone.

The realm of spirit is your world too. You're connected to it. The loving energy of spirit is there to help you. And you can make it part of your everyday life when you seek out their counsel and accept their love. With your invitation you create love when you ask to bring love and wisdom into your life. And anything's possible. A spirit's path is intricate and as limitless as creation. And spiritual language, the way spirit talks to us, is fascinating and beautiful. Through associations, inspirations, and timing, they direct our lives. They show us that our problems aren't life's tragedies. They're its glory and the reflection of spirit's triumph over life's resistance.

Certainly, ceremonies are appreciated by spirit. That's one of the values religious practice gives us. Prayerful ceremonies act as the physical gifts we give to recognize the spirit world. These are the gifts of acknowledgment and gratitude. Your gratitude strengthens and energizes this relationship, increases your awareness, and helps to clarify the guidance. It's not a requirement though. Every moment your thoughts naturally reach out to them. Your intentions touch them and their love returns to you in kind. And there's never a schedule so you can't be late.

WHAT IF YOU CAN'T DO IT?

Don't waste your time worrying about failure. While that's proverbially "easier said than done," look at the reality in life. Every day our lives hold on by the thinnest of threads. With every breath we challenge and overcome death. Life's that fragile. Yet we thrive here. Just staying alive is a bigger challenge than any setback might mean. It's a wonder we survive here at all. Even cultures living in the harshest conditions find ways to survive their circumstances as part of their daily existence. They have to live. And they learn how to do it whether it's in the frozen Arctic or the parched deserts of Africa. Every day God supports them in their strenuous existence. And likewise God supports you in your existence too.

A New Freedom

We live at a unique time in human history. It crystallizes in America's ideal of personal freedom. It's the freedom of peace through power. It's the freedom of abundance through wealth. It's the freedom of resources through science. It's the freedom of time through technology. It's the freedom of action through law, information through the media, and knowledge through history. It's the freedom of service through civilization. And it joins in the freedom of individuality for everyone to use as they see fit. That's the freedom to love.

But the freedom of individuality can degenerate into, "It's easy. I can do it by myself and I don't need you so I don't have to respect you." It's the illusion that the structure of civilization alone is all that anyone needs to be successful. That if you learn its rules you can take anything you want from it. Then people don't matter. Today's struggles are with our thoughts and feelings, not the physical challenges which dominated earlier generations. Modern success has made us younger but has it taken us any farther? Youth must develop the matching character it needs to move forward. It's still about survival though. And it's as critical as it ever was.

Today we're close to a divine breakthrough for civilization. It's about adding more love to our lives. We're no longer preoccupied with survival as the sole reason of our day. More than ever before, many of us partake in the full spectrum of life's possibilities. And the past is part of the design. It's brought us to where we are today. Now it's time to take the next step. The new challenge is deciding where we're going from here and how to do it.

LET GOD DO IT.

There's a tendency to trivialize God. We minimize God as a part of our lives instead of seeing God as the reason for it. So God becomes nothing more than a celebrity. We honor God but we don't know why. We expect something from God but we don't know what. We feel a debt to God but we don't know how to repay it. God's the highest of something but we can't quite describe it.

So to accept God's messengers we've humanized them. But unless we see them as representing God; Jesus, Mohammed, Moses, and all the many others seem dismissible. And it's only when you see God's love in the gift of these beautiful being's presence on our planet that you include yourself in God's love for it.

Who you are matters. Your personal contribution magnifies society. On every planet in the universe, in spirit we're all the same. We share physical nature. We share the same concepts in God's imagination. And though our experiences are as different as a forest hermit's life is to that of a big city dweller, we share the same expectations. We all have needs and wants and joys. And we all know love. The family of consciousness is your family too. And it guides all species with the same spiritual heartbeat you have.

God's love has no superiors. It's a blessing on all creation. So the love that guides the universe guides you too—no matter what your challenges are. So fill yourself with it often. Feed on it! Aspire to it! Make it your number one priority and you'll always be halfway home. Let your life be fulfilled through love. That's your blessing.

Think About It — Chapter 1

Thought #1:   The purpose of hardship is to make us stronger and wiser, and to prove to ourselves that we're infinitely greater than any challenge.

Thought #2:   Knowledge is our survival on this planet. It should be sought out, appreciated, and respected.

Thought #3:   Building your life takes time.

Thought #4:   We all possess opportunity.

Thought #5:   Being open to your spiritual dimension can help you immensely.

Thought #6:   Throughout the universe every species knows love.

POSITIVE ENERGY CREATES
POSITIVE RESULTS.
THAT'S WHY IT'S ESSENTIAL
TO IDENTIFY YOUR GOOD FEELINGS
AND KNOW WHAT MAKES
YOU HAPPY.

IT'S IMPORTANT TO BE HONEST
WITH YOURSELF.
THE TRUTH OF YOUR INNER BEING
WILL DRIVE YOU
TO THE FUTURE THAT REFLECTS
WHO YOU ARE.

CHAPTER 2

THe ReaSoN WHy

So what are you supposed to do? What are you supposed to want? What's right? What's right supposed to feel like? How will you know when it feels right? What does wrong feel like? Who'll tell you the difference? What if you mix them up? Who'll show you how to do it? Who should you ask? When? Why? Damn, it's scary!

It's all very confusing. And your sense of self-awareness comes when you just have limited experience to deal with it. But like it or not the timing is perfect as each inescapable stage of life must be.

WHAT'S IMPORTANT TO YOU?

As a new adult you're entering a time when you have to decide for yourself the values you'll live by. And you'll have to learn how to get along with others too. So how do you create a balance you'll accept that lets you live in harmony with your neighbors? And once you choose a perspective that's fair you'll need proof to give your values vitality to trust them.

More than that, it takes a lifetime to grasp the peculiarities forced on you by the variety in life's circumstances. Life is endlessly intricate and constantly changing. It's all around you with you in the middle. It's like an astronaut carnival ride that turns you in one direction while it spins you in another at the same time.

At this point in your life choosing your values is all theoretical. It takes years of experience to give you a stable platform of life affirming values. But to start you can get your direction from the rules of social order where you live. Those are the laws, regulations, and courtesies developed by a community to make life easier for everyone. The confusing part is when you see everyone in society has their own interpretation of what the limits mean and who the limits should affect. And the answers change because the issues float on the tide of a community's desires. So it's normal to question ourselves. *When should we stay with our current values? When should we push the limits of those values? And when should we revise our values with new ones?*

You can begin by examining the values of those close to you—your friends, family, teachers, people you work with, and your acquaintances. In the end though you'll decide your own values. And you'll do it well, to the best of your ability, regardless of the uncertainties or inevitable mistakes. You'll choose one thing or the other, one way or another, and what's important to you or not. They're your choices to make and you'll make them.

But if you hold off because your afraid, even the decision to do nothing can be turned to your advantage. Through the simplest thought to move forward you can succeed by faith alone if you let yourself accept God's guidance.

Whatever you do or don't do, the world will move forward in its divine state of chaos with people feeling every minute like they're riding a wild horse for the first time. And you're part of it, moving with it wherever it goes. So hold on tight, pay attention, and learn to control it. People are regularly good at it. Learn from those who've been there before and you'll be good at it too. Anyone who's been successful in life at one time was just like you. They had to learn how.

SPIRITING AROUND EXERCISE:

Revealing Your Nature

To help you understand yourself, magazines and newspaper classified ads are good tools to help you see what your values are when you're having trouble identifying them. Which items do you like? Which jobs catch your interest? Which activities appeal to you? Which house? Which car? Which place? Which style? Mark the ads and think about them. What do you like about them? Why? Be honest with yourself even if it doesn't sound right. Ask yourself why it doesn't sound right. Then raise it to the next level in your mind. What would you do if you had it? Let that be the trigger for exploring who you are. And let it guide you to your possibilities.

But don't judge yourself by the ads. There are no wrong answers. Your only criterion is that you enjoy what you like. There's your truth. When you're honest with yourself and love who you are, you're on your way to having what you want.

WHO ARE YOU?

With assessing your values you'll need to take inventory of yourself. That means identifying your personality. Where are your strengths? What are your shortcomings? Which shortcomings could be eliminated by working on them? Which ones do you have to work around? How can you increase your abilities? You need to take a big non-judgmental look at yourself to evaluate the tools in your toolbox. It's your starting point for understanding yourself.

It's essential to be fair and honest with yourself and include everything. That's the truth of it. The more you know who you are, without comparing yourself to others, will give you more confidence. You'll know what you like and you'll like yourself for it. And the more confident you feel, the sooner you'll be on your way to having what you want. You'll see what helps or hinders you, you'll eliminate deficiencies, and you'll see the possibilities in what you already have.

You should question yourself knowing that you'll find the answers even if you have to hunt for them. Start by describing your current circumstances. Then in your mind make the changes you'd like. Be honest with yourself. Ignoring the truth won't change it. But accepting the truth gives you power over it.

With a good look at yourself you'll see how your personality deals with life. And you'll see that there are others like you too. And thinking about them can give you more insight into your own possibilities.

You can speak to others with the same or even an opposite attitude and explore how they think and feel about things. What's their attitude meant to them? What do they like about it? Has it ever caused them any problems? It's not accuracy you're looking for because they might not understand it any more than you do. They do have their own perspective though. And they have a valid perspective from their own life experience that can help you see the patterns and consistencies we share in nature's movements.

And accept that disabilities and peculiarities are there to help you. The world is not your judge. Only you and God know what's right for you. Nature gives you life. And here everyone is perfect unto themselves and God.

Everything that makes you who you are is an asset. Once you believe that, you can use it to your advantage. When you accept the parts of you that are problematic you can achieve an emotional balance that helps you overcome your problems. If you ignore or reject any part of yourself, you reduce your potential for self-acceptance. Self-acceptance is the basis for self-respect. And self-respect is the expression of self-love that transcends the mass conscious identity we all depend on for security. Real security is being your own person while your self-acceptance lets your identity flourish.

SPiRiTiNG ҀROUND EXERCiSE:

It Depends on the Circumstances.

Character features don't matter till the situation's considered. Whether something's a strength or a weakness is only revealed by what you're trying to do. So here's something to do to get a better picture of yourself. First list all your traits. That's everything you can think about yourself. Are you short or tall? Are you a quick thinker or more deliberate? Are you friendly and outgoing or more private? Are you self-important or self-effacing? Are you patient or emotional? What do you do for fun? What kind of work do you like? Are you educated for what you want to do? List as much as you can but don't judge anything. It's not a commentary on your value as a person. It's an explanation of who you are. Remember whatever details make you who you are, their quality are determined by how you use them.

YOU'RE THE BiGGEST INFLUENCE ON YOUR LiFE.

If any old situation is good enough for you then that's exactly what you'll get. You'll always be living some unexpected situation without any plan. And you'll be solving useless problems just to stay in the same undefined place. You can do better than that. SO DECIDE TO DO IT!

There's order to life. And you should expect favorable or unfavorable changes according to predictable paths. You can expect people to act in reasonably predictable ways. And knowing that, you can prepare for what might happen. You can have a plan ready regardless of the direction life takes you.

Advertising's based on the same principle. Advertisers have learned how to influence people and motivate them to buy their products and services. It might not be an immediate need they solve but when the time comes the seed's been planted. There's a direction already in place. You can use the same concept. You can influence the paths these natural events follow by setting clear goals for yourself. And then let your goals lead you along the same paths.

You should develop a non-judgmental honest sensitivity to your present situation. Know where you are and know which changes could best move you forward to where you want to be. It's like a chess game. Your anticipation of the possibilities combined with your knowledge of the rules gives you the best opportunity to make things happen the way you want them to.

And it's important to regularly evaluate your situation. Then you'll be aware of the current conditions in your changing world. And you'll see if where you stand has changed. You'll know the current identity of the circumstances that define your life. For example, you might be working somewhere with new employees joining the company while others are leaving. Customers or their needs can change. So the work you do changes to accommodate them. Or new technologies come and change the way you do things. As you gain experience you're more effective at your job. That gives you more time to do other things. Everything changes. Your co-workers' personal problems, your health, and even the weather affect those changes. You see the picture. It's a moving picture and you're in it.

You're a part of the picture and it's going to affect you. But by accepting the picture and knowing it affects you, you can be ready for each new day. The lesson is you can create opportunities when you anticipate your needs.

CHESS — MORE THAN JUST A GAME

Chess is an excellent teacher. It shows you how to think ahead for the future. It teaches you to anticipate the changing places of the pieces. By planning ahead you'll see how relationships change and possibilities move in predictable patterns.

Chess teaches that individual choices give multiple results. It demonstrates how you create different outcomes by the different moves you make. So it shows how your actions, reactions, and reactions to reactions can move you forward to different futures.

Still, predicting the future isn't easy. It's the variety of alternatives created by every new move that makes it hard. But the bottom line is you can protect yourself from dangers and put yourself in a better place to take advantage of opportunities when you foresee them.

Evaluating the results of your choices in relation to your goals is part of any endeavor. They're the links that connect you to your future. And the strength of each link is important because it supports the whole chain. Every choice you make matters because it passes its vitality along the entire length of the chain and helps it to grow.

WHAT ARE YOUR GOALS?

Goals are simple to define. It's what you want. It's your desired result. It's your objective. It's where you want to be. It's the situation you hope for. And it's the things you want to own. It's a relationship between you and life that has to be satisfied. You can identify these feelings as your inner desire. It's your passion seeking comfort. It's the words, "I want that!" "That's for me!" "That's mine!" It's the sense that you just have to have it. And you know that you'll suffer till it's yours. You think about it all the time. And joyous relief comes in your achievement.

But how will you know you have what you really want? YOU have to decide. YOU have to make up your mind. YOU have to choose from the events, possibilities, relationships, paths, responsibilities, situations, and everything else that's out there. It's only up to you to pick out what you like.

It's important to see things being perfect, happening just the way you like. Then you have to ask yourself some questions. How do you get there? Where can you go once you've been there? Where do you want to go? And what could change it? Then ask again and again all the way to your future.

Now your goals exist as a loose collection of dreams, desires, and intentions. They're specific things that on some level you know you want. They're attractive to you. But maturity shows that goals can change shape and importance as you explore them. And life's events change too. So your goals can bounce off new situations in unexpected ways. Learning to handle it all is like training to be a juggler. It takes patience, practice, and believing you'll succeed.

No matter how jumbled up things seem, the laser beam straightness of your happiness knows who you are. And it'll guide you through life's endless questions. Remember that your vision of the future is more than a description of how you want things to be. It's the path that gets you there. So sincerity empowers you. Happiness is your guide. And honesty will be your independence.

SPIRITING AROUND EXERCISE:

Just What You Always Wanted

Think about the qualities that define your happiness. Make a list. Then pick the ones you like the best. It could be a new job or to live somewhere special, to find a sweetheart or meet a new friend, or to do something that's always fascinated you. It could even be something no one's ever done before. In time you'll get to know yourself. And when you focus on yourself, beyond the lockstep disarray of mass consciousness, you refine your maturity. It's easier than you think.

GOALS & MOMENTUM

When you subconsciously see your goals it releases your creativity. And when you focus your thoughts on a particular goal your whole psyche turns to face it. It's like a spotlight was shined on your goal. It attracts your attention. And as your true desire it energizes every part of you. It's the power of your satisfaction striving to realize itself. And the more desire you aim at a goal, the more defined it becomes. So your clarity feeds on itself. And as it eliminates unrelated details, your excitement increases.

It's like a sports team executing a play in perfect sync. Each player is an individual with a clear idea of their job but joined with the others on the team they're driven by a common purpose. They all want the same thing. They want to win the game. They want to win the championship. Everyone wants to be a champion. Everyone wants to succeed.

It's the same way things happen in your own life. Every atom of your being comes together in a common purpose. In your unity your power grows and your progress can achieve more. And it's through this efficiency that you create opportunities for yourself as nature responds to your honest intentions.

Positive energy creates positive results. That's why it's essential for you to look inside yourself to identify your good feelings and realize what makes you happy. That's why it's important to be honest with yourself. It's the subtlety of your inner being that's the determiner of your heart's desires. And there may be parts of you much closer to your goals than you think. Faith stimulates progress and positive actions make things happen. This energy supports your sincerity because in your honesty exists the part of you that's real and whole with the universe.

With self-awareness and clear goals a synergy takes place. Your intentions and efforts join together. What you once thought was unachievable might be waiting for you right outside your door. You may see an impossibility of the past is now an indivisible part of your nature. And you might now see that it's always been a part of you that you just had to learn how to realize.

THE BREAKAWAY

So how do you break from your current situation? Do you know where you want to go? What has to change to get you there? Should you be patient or do something now? Think about it. Are all your considerations important to your goal? Are there any distractions that are wasting your time? You may already have what you need. Maybe just your direction has to change. Or sometimes the right path takes you somewhere else first.

It takes personal development to get what you want from life. And you create the means to control it. You build your confidence and that makes things happen. You gain the courage to admit what you don't know and learn what you need to know. And as you accept your personal responsibility, you mature. But there are many things that affect growing up. From race and gender to nationality, family, and economic conditions, the world asks a lot from us. It's complex, compelling, and confusing. There's a lot going on within and around you that affects you. It's just the way life is. But whatever happens, your sincerity guarantees you'll do well regardless of the situation.

THE BARRIERS

Your plans should be flexible because your path has infinite possibilities. And there are always hurdles to clear. You might be surprised to know that sometimes we unconsciously undermine our own happiness. So watch out for the warning signs because we entertain endless techniques for sabotaging ourselves. They're similar but different for everyone because our creativity gives us infinite variety in the details. These ideas create unnecessary prerequisites for your success. They modify reality and unfairly qualify your progress. They have no affect on the outcome other than the way their restrictive nature limits your possibilities. This is the concept of "UNLESS…"

Conditional Thinking

Unfortunately we all have a tendency to limit ourselves with conditional thoughts. But we cripple our success when we bind it to unnecessary criteria. If we preface some circumstance with, "It must be this way to start." or "Unless it finishes exactly like that," then we're restricting our thoughts and feelings about the right way to do something. And we create mountains to climb that are only real in our imaginations.

For example, you might not let yourself surpass a level of achievement beyond what you think you deserve. So you judge yourself and design limiting barriers that block your success.

Conditional thinking can be about anything. It takes the form of, "Unless this happens first then that can't happen." So you tell yourself, "Unless you have the right clothes you won't fit in." "Unless you have more money it isn't possible." "Unless you're the right race you won't be included. Or the right religion, or the right body shape, or the right hair color, unless..., unless..., unless..." Unless whatever pre-described condition you identify with happens then you can't have what you want. Or unless it's a certain way or in a specific order then it's not right or it can't be done. Forget that! Do what's best for you. Don't use conditions as an excuse. It's always possible.

It's also unfortunate that these mental restrictions can enter your psyche and settle in the cellular structure of your body. There, inter-acting with your body's cellular web, they can influence your entire life. They can impose subtle restraints on your mental, physical, and emotional consciousness. They can change your attitude from positive to negative or force you into thoughts conforming to their limits. Your opinion of your well-being is reflected out to the world where you meet it every day in your challenges. And trusting that conditional thoughts have no real power over you is where you start healing your confidence.

As conditional thinking affects the way you understand yourself it also affects your health. Physical burdens may not be consciously intentional but they can develop out of the simple defenses your mind designed to help you deal with life. Like physical pains in your body, mental and emotional pains can reside in your body and come up at any time. To make the pain go away, sometimes we suppress it and bury it away in some dark corner of our minds. But then instead of using it to heal ourselves we may become frightened of our own thoughts and feelings. And we deny ourselves. But even if you can control a painful thought by the strength of your will, the relief is temporary because that suffering remains inside you. Without your acceptance, that underlying suffering continues in all its confusion. And it can rise up without warning to darken your mood. Even the faintest hint of some past conflict can affect what you're feeling today.

So pay attention to your feelings. Don't ignore your emotional pains. Even when it hurts, feel it! That's how you identify them. Your goal is to release those old hurts so they can't bother you anymore. You need to accept the feelings you once avoided which left you emotionally unresolved. It takes mature personality skills to deal with uncomfortable feelings. And there's no time knowing when you'll have them.

But now is the time to fix it. You can do the work to heal your emotions, clear out the negative thoughts that supported your pain, and make sense of your life. Don't worry if it's hard. It's going to reveal the instability in your beliefs. But even though you're turning things upside down, you have to trust the process and have faith that you'll be successful. You'll feel better as you go because there's comfort in the truth. And there really is no other way.

Your experiences demonstrate the direction of your purpose. And when you're honest with yourself you can see how your subconscious thoughts directed your life. You'll see how they characterized every plan you've ever had and the preconditions they required. Then you can remove the ones you don't like. And unencumbered by limiting thoughts, many of life's problems are reduced to sensible actions which succeed in their own natural way.

But you don't have to suffer while you're searching your soul for your inner truth. Just love every part of yourself. You're your primary responsibility. So always be fair to yourself. There's a core to you that emanates the truth through everything you do. It's the clear intelligence where your thoughts, emotions, beliefs, and sensations surround you. This is the immaculate part of you that evaluates your experience. You're always doing the best you can. And I hope this book can help you do it better.

Life's flexibility exists for your success. So if it's right for you, go for it. Any self-constraints beyond that are false. They either exist as self-created misconceptions or they've been imposed on you from some outside source that's misguided about what's important to you. You have the power to eliminate the limitations of conditional thinking. With your freedom you'll release enormous amounts of unburdened energy that can help you towards your goals. And your confidence will soar when you accept the power you've always had and see the weakness in the resistance that had you trapped.

Effort over Ease

We sabotage ourselves when we choose the easy way instead of doing what's right. What's right isn't hard or easy. It's accepting what has to be done. So there's no reason to struggle with it if you don't like it. You just do it. For instance, without seeing the value in work you might not tolerate it. You might avoid working and see yourself as a "victim of work." You might see yourself as a victim of the system. But until you find a better way you'll have to rely on what's available to support yourself. Or if you're a student you might see yourself as a victim of a system that forces you to study things you find boring. And you may suffer through it without the satisfaction that balances your time with good value. Certainly, having to do something you don't like can be frustrating. It can make you feel weak and disappointed in yourself. And you can feel helpless because you're not doing what you really want to do.

As a better choice it's wise to consider there could be benefits in dissatisfying situations. So it's important to acknowledge that your immaturity may be what's blocking you from seeing the advantages in your situation. Know that all situations are temporary. If you see them as stepping stones and essential to your goals then they can be the steps that create the road to your happiness. Problems are easier to handle when you know that your happiness is at the end of the road, not just the endless suffering you may imagine from your present situation. Time passes and you'll mature. And bad times and their painful memories will gradually fade away. So don't waste your suffering being bitter, angry, and frustrated with life's unfairness. You pay a high price for your experience so use it. Think about it. Learn from it. Use it to make your life better. It's up to you to give your experiences value by seeing the benefits in them. And your patient consideration will guide you to get the most out of everything you've paid for.

See your life for its potential. You'll grow up and set your own course someday. Keep your problems small and respect your responsibilities. Don't suffer any more than you have to. Do your best. Look to the future but know your next step. Be enthusiastic but keep your goals in sight. Enthusiasm blends your intentions with emotion. It excites your creativity. And here creativity means that you're human. There God resides in your intuition. And that intuition stirs your mind into action. Your plans give it focus. And that focus forces your goals to form. Your knowledge recycles and each cycle moves you closer to what you want. But it takes its own time. And sometimes the only comfort you'll have is to know that you're moving forward. So to be really successful you must intuitively feel it.

Don't quit where you are now. Exploit your present circumstances for the value you find there. If you can't be your best, then be the best you can. And don't let temporary circumstances prevent you from excelling on your own terms. You'll find a way and you'll be helped along the way. Conditions change to force our growth. And while life's hectic pace may obscure it, we grow with it every day. And growth means that new opportunities are always happening for you.

Maturity is self-reliance. So success is your choice. It's in doing what you believe in that you prove your responsibility to life. So review your beliefs and dismiss, revise, or accept them. They're the part of you you'll rely on.

You're always at the beginning so you can never be behind. So there's never a need to rush and catch up with the crowd. We all want to do better. But you can be conscious about it. Then you're in control and your life is yours. You deserve it. You have no debts to anyone. And you don't exist because of anyone. Your mandate comes from God. You're a fully authorized individual with the responsibility to express yourself as the person you are.

Other People's Influence

Sometimes self-sabotage is a reaction to other people's misinterpretations which guide us even when those beliefs conflict with our own feelings and common sense. That faulty guidance permeates a fertile young consciousness. And it colors many of the early judgments a person makes about life.

Insidiously, as a seed in a developing mind, misguided support can create future problems. And it's not just inexperienced child-rearing that's the issue. It's the subconscious misgivings on life and thoughts on social conduct passed along with the loving guidance.

The people you see every day, your human neighborhood, have the greatest effect on your beliefs. Your school, religion, work, ethnic group, age group, country, and the whole mass consciousness of the planet are all firmly joined in imposing a point of view on you. But those closest to you, the ones you trust the most, will always have the greatest influence on what you believe.

As a result you'll have conflicts. Something's going to feel good but you'll avoid it because someone impressed on you it was bad. So you may try to eliminate the conflict by giving in, hoping to avoid being attacked or rejected. Maybe the last time you expressed happiness, expecting support, you found disapproval. So to avoid unpleasant feelings you gave up on your happiness and sacrificed your joy to a dull truce. You might rationalize it. Or you may suffer, uncomfortable with the circumstances and confused by the question, "Why can't you be happy?" It's because you've sacrificed something that should never be given up in any situation—the joy of your free spirit.

It's important to know when someone's beliefs conflict with your own inner wisdom. And even if you can't do anything about it, you can protect your desires in your hopes. And you can develop the patience and confidence to honor your dreams while you're still wise enough to respect someone else's point of view. And you can do it without anyone's overbearing attitude creating doubts for you about what your happiness should mean. Eliminating this kind of needless suffering begins and ends with you.

Be open to suggestions but check your sources carefully. Everyone has their own agenda. What someone thinks is good for them might not be right for you. While it's worthwhile to see other points of view, it's also important to question their motives, evaluate their experiences, and consider their mood. And it's important to question your responsibility to the trust others put in you when you give them advice as well.

KNOWLEDGE BY ASSOCIATION

While other people's approval isn't needed, they do have important insights. And a great way to learn is by observing someone doing something that interests you. You can learn a lot watching people meet their challenges and seeing what results. And by evaluating their choices it becomes a part of you. So you can be more than sympathetic. You can be objective. And that can be the tool you use to fix your own problems or build your future.

Remember to be clear on what's happening and fair to those involved. See how each perspective is supported. Then remove the partialities. Once the truth is revealed, you can use your own values to decide what's right.

Don't dismiss anything without giving it a second thought. There could be seeds of wisdom in the most confusing advice when you take the time to think about it. But even with the help you get you still judge your own life. So, be discerning. Refine the truth from what you find. And trust yourself. You're eminently reliable.

MENTORiNG: A SHORT CUT

You can find a mentor. It shows maturity because it recognizes that you have a lot to learn. It's a popular concept and can be very rewarding. And you don't have to be in school or some corporate business environment to benefit from working with a mentor. It just has to be someone who'll help you who has more knowledge and experience than you do.

A mentor is someone with wisdom tuned through experience. And the person should be generous and look forward to sharing their insights with you. You'd want to pick someone with experience that interests you. But that doesn't exclude "everything about life" if that's what's most important to you. They can also help you with introductions to people who could be valuable to your future.

With a mentor, what's important is the guidance that comes from their years of correcting mistakes, exploiting successes, and weighing the price they paid for them. They can expose your priorities and show you how they stand the test of time. They've seen how experiences evolve. And they can identify your talents and advise you which you can improve.

Mentors can be excellent. They give you an objective point of view. They have no investment to protect like a family member who might expect something in return. There's nothing wrong with advice coming from a loving relationship but it can limit itself when it tries to protect the relationship at the expense of good guidance. Then the hard advice, which in the long run would strengthen you, gets lost.

An objective mentor can give you a safe forum for your thoughts. So you can let your thoughts express freely without the fear of judgment. Without this sanctuary you might hold in your feelings and shield yourself from the limiting thoughts of a loving but misguided family member.

FROM THE PAST

Historical observations are the foundation for self-exploration. It's the reassurance that others have gone here before you. They may have come by different roads but their goals were likely the same as yours. So by knowing the past you can gain insight into the connections that make up your life today.

Seeing the results of history's choices reveals humanity's central themes. And it provides a valuable perspective on your own search for happiness. The best part is that so many have gone before you. And they've left behind in their art and writings a record for you to use.

So it's almost certain that you'll discover someone like yourself who looked at things the same way you do. Their mind will resonate with yours. You'll understand them. So find them. Learn from what they left for you. Because we all walk the same path with the same lessons someone else has already learned.

Don't be concerned if some famous figure turns out to be boring or confusing. Don't waste your time. You can learn about them later if you want. There are plenty of others you'll like because they've written right to your soul's understanding.

The considerations for choosing a mentor should include their patience, compassion, resolve, knowledge, experience, common sense, and generosity. With that they'll do fine by you. And with reciprocal respect you'll do fine by them. But what will they ask in return? You'll satisfy them with your success. You'll love them with your remembrance. And you'll honor them with the exemplary character that shines through you as a beacon to the possibilities of trust and commitment.

A PERSONAL RESPONSIBILITY

Self-determination is your decision. It's your job. Every psychic part of you—your thoughts, feelings, predilections, talents, abilities, natural gifts, and joys—demand one thing from you. Leadership!

But don't worry. You're ready to be a leader. Despite what you think you're missing, you have everything you need right now to be successful. And your disbelief doesn't change it. If you think you can't do it, you're wrong. You can do it! And you will do it.

No matter the gender, age, race, religion, or background; life's the same for all of us. It's God's plan and the plan never fails. And don't worry that you have to wait too long to get what you want because you won't have to wait forever. Remember, God's waiting with you.

Wherever you are you control your happiness. So trust yourself. Trust yourself and only yourself. Trust your feelings, trust your thoughts, and trust your judgment. Think deliberately and act decisively. Thinking things through is a positive action. It's part of the process. Considering how to do things better is the first step to doing things right. It takes time to manifest who you really are. But right thinking has no schedule.

SOME UNUSUAL FRiENDS

As surprising as it sounds and as unlikely as it seems, your worst feelings—fear, guilt, anger, and sorrow—are your friends. And they're there to help you. And it's possible to love every part of yourself…even those feelings that make you uncomfortable. You can love your negative feelings in the same way they've always loved you. Like loyal soldiers; fear, guilt, anger, and sorrow protect you when you can't protect yourself. Their only reason for being is to stand by you. They react automatically. When you don't know what to think, what to say, or what to do, those feelings come to defend you. But it can give you a feeling of being out of control when they react faster than your thoughts do. But that's why you need them. You lead them though and they wait patiently to be dismissed. They love you and they'll always love you. But it's time to retire your old trusted friends. But first they must believe that you'll be okay without them. You have to prove that you've developed your confidence to the point where you can love yourself unconditionally. As your positive consciousness takes shape you can release those old negative feelings. Then they'll recede, joyfully giving you back the responsibility for your own self-protection. And as you mature they'll go away to leave only positive feelings of confidence filling your life.

When fear goes, defenselessness takes its place and love may enter. When anger goes, patience takes its place and love may enter. When sorrow goes, hope takes its place and love may enter. And when guilt goes, forgiveness takes its place and love may enter. So release those emotions with gratitude for their service to you. Love them as a part of you. And love them for their devotion because they were always there to help you. Then they'll leave knowing they did a good job when you needed them.

BELiEVE IN YOURSELF.

To believe in yourself you must take that "Leap of Faith." It's inevitable that you'll move beyond the temporary obstacles caused by low self-esteem. Know that self-loathing doesn't exist in reality. It's a concept you've accepted. And the conditions that gave you the idea don't matter. True, it's thoughts you have about yourself but it's not your fault. Self-criticism is a normal reaction to life's relentless pressures. But it has to be fair and honest if it's going to support your improvement.

While self-doubts are just opinions, they're the most important opinions in the world. They're your opinions about yourself. And with a positive outlook your thoughts and feelings can be changed for the better. Like the Bible passage that says, "Real faith even as small as a mustard seed is enough to move mountains." the seed of your decision to love yourself can mature into an everlasting faith in the universe's inherent desire to help you succeed.

Faith isn't your determination to overcome your difficulties. It's your soul's desire to succeed. It's not despising a part of yourself you hope another part of you can defeat. There are no bad parts to you. Faith accepts all of you. We all have parts of ourselves we'd like to heal so we can enjoy our lives better. Faith trusts the certainty of healing and creates a positive environment for it. Faith's the medicine that heals our personalities and gives rest to our souls.

Whatever happens, know that you'll do better. And trust your trust in God. That's where it all begins. That's where you'll feel your confidence inspired by God's commitment. Your situation might not change immediately but you can encourage yourself knowing there's always a solution waiting for you.

As your trust grows you'll see positive things happen in your life. You'll develop a common sense wisdom in harmony with life. And you'll see life resonate it back to you. You're never alone. You're always interacting with a willing world of spirit wanting to help you. And together we give reality to God's purpose.

GOD'S THE WAY TO A FULL LIFE.

The spiritual world exists and you're a part of it. You're whole with it and everything it has is yours. That means you can consciously access your spiritual wisdom. From there you can see how common sense, your master key for living, lets you do anything you want. It's the magic you've always wanted. So take another look at it. Then decide for yourself if spirit is real or if the billions of people worshiping God are just foolish.

But it seems distant and vaguely explained at best. Is there a higher power that knows the truth about life while we're still guessing at it? Does some greater power really oversee our lives? We've been debating that idea since we became aware of ourselves. And our peace of mind demands an answer. But that's the puzzle of life's meaning. A part of us knows there's something there. It's intelligent but somehow wiser than our thoughts. You can feel its presence in the meaning of events beyond any outcome. And it speaks lovingly to you when you let it.

SO HOW'S IT BETTER?

Completeness is found in spirit. That's why worshiping quantity, the philosophy that more is better, gives only temporary satisfaction. Quality in living isn't about who has the most. It's about having enough of *what's important to you*. That's the place in ourselves where we all want satisfaction.

So we imitate it by trying to be the best looking, doing the wildest things, or knowing the coolest thing to say. We want to be the smartest, own the best stuff, or be the most popular. We use what's handy and tangible, things we think we control, to fill that empty part of ourselves. We mistakenly think we can solve the infinite truth of our lives with some emotional Band-Aid we exalt beyond its ability. So we paint over the parts of ourselves we don't like to see. But then we miss out on the beautiful mosaic that reveals our true selves.

Emotional patches are eventually revealed as cosmetic repairs and not the real answer to happiness. Instead, try seeing your life as a spiritual obstacle course meant to exercise your soul and build up your spirit. Your answer to success is supported by your spiritual outlook.

DOES iT REALLY WORK?

If you need an extraordinary event to prove God's presence, forget it. If everything you see in life isn't enough to prove that something greater than what you see with your senses is at work here then nothing will. Slow down a minute and think about the endless phenomena here. How it all comes together in graceful perfection. Everything acts on everything else and it all joins together in infinite possibilities. A forest can stand where a tree once grew and any newborn can be tomorrow's astronaut.

Spirit doesn't produce results on demand. But they can happen with miraculous speed when those results are part of your soul's development. And the process contains your guidance in the spiritual root of your problems. When a problem is understood and eliminated at its root then it's gone forever. And like a garden cleared of weeds so can your discontent be healed. It's important because we often focus on just solving our immediate problems. And those may be only symptoms of a deeper want.

YOU DON'T BELiEVE iT?

We all want relief NOW! And we often don't care what it is as long as it's fast. Like weeding a garden though, you have to get down on your knees and pull hard to get the weeds out. You have to get your hands dirty. It's not just trimming the weed where you see it. And a fast fix, while it seems the easiest, is often the most difficult and time-consuming way to solve a problem. Eventually, it's just a distraction. It rarely solves anything and you condemn yourself to small periods of passing comfort. It becomes a pattern of fix and re-fix till you make that commitment to fix the problem right, once, and for all.

Negative thoughts are like that. Like weeds, even as a seed, they exist in their entirety. And they can easily grow back where you don't want them. If they don't belong in your garden, they burden it. They drain you of the energy you give to support them. They're false trails so they waste your time. But take away their power and they disappear. So whatever you have to do to eliminate negative thoughts, you just have to do it.

FiNALLY!

The best way for doing anything is the right way. It may not be the fastest or the cheapest way. Things are as easy as they are. Your achievement has its requirements. And they have to be complete for you to be satisfied. Easy or hard aren't the criteria. Hard doesn't know what to do. So, learn how to do it. And easy is just a matter of time. So, take the time you need. It's only your soul's fulfillment that can bring you peace and happiness.

There's some sense in this brittle reality. And your challenges don't mean there's some fault in your soul. They do show responsibility though. And the evidence that you're alive and working through your problems proves that you're fulfilling your responsibilities. Spirit sees this with compassion for you. Creation honors your efforts on its behalf. They can't be separated. In every moment of your life you're part of a great miracle. Your growth is cared for and appreciated. You're important. You experience your existence in your own unique way. And the universe loves you for it because when you feed your experience into Creation love grows everywhere.

BE ON THE ALERT FOR MESSAGES FROM SPIRIT.

Spiritual wisdom finds ways to communicate with us through the busy-ness of our demanding lives. Using everything from religious ceremonies to the common cold, God sends us daily messages of serenity and redemption. Whether in the images of your dreams or the revelations of a child's remark, these messages stir your mind to spark your soul's wisdom. And it's as much inside you as it could be from an outside event. It can be as simple as your choice to make a right turn instead of a left or get gas before going to the bank instead of the other way around. The world turns on exquisite timing where a simple decision can change the rest of your life. And there's really nothing you can do about it. That's a message too.

So the seed of every moment holds your future. What looks like a casual choice can have you running into an old friend by being in the right place at the right time or being delayed and missing something important because you're in the wrong place at the wrong time.

That's how fragile the structure of our lives is. It's a structure we think we can dominate though. We think we can make ourselves stronger than life if we exercise enough or drive the trendiest car. But it's the seemingly small ways God touches our lives that really affect us.

And other than being at peace with life there's really little you can do to affect it. You can't plan anything so perfectly that you won't come up empty-handed. And you'll never be so lost that life can't spin around and give you everything you've ever wanted. The connections you make are coincidental but they're not arbitrary. They have purpose. They're the gears in God's grand plan for you.

The one thing you can do is sensitize yourself to the plan by knowing it exists. Then look for patterns and repetitions in life's events. Learn from the similarities. These are the messages intended to attract your attention. This is Spirit calling out to you in the physical world and highlighting what can help you. These messages alert you to life's potentials and include within their form the meaning of their resolution.

Whether it's "on a silver platter" or "a written invitation," we should accept that certain events are God's guidance for what's happening in our lives. And it's not always something extreme that'll be your "wake up call." It's because there are blessings in those challenges when we cast our eyes to the sky and beg God, "Why me?" The real question is, "Dear God, in your grace and greatness, why are you creating this in my life? What do you want me to see?"

Everyone somehow questions their existence. And like everything else in life its core is understandable. While it's obscure, it's not meant to be hidden. It's only disguised enough so it can be discovered with a little effort. And when we get too far from it we're given clues to its presence. But you don't have to start your search as a blank slate.

You can start from a point where history's greatest minds have already been. Their discoveries are yours for the reading. It's like them saying, "I've already been there. Now you take it from here." Their journey is your journey. And it reaches out from every life there ever was to every life there will ever be. It's because everyone's purpose is the same. To live God's love.

Don't worry that you'll miss something. You'll never miss anything that's important to you. It's impossible. It's more likely you'll be the first one to know something. Like a magnet, you attract what you need. That includes knowing everything that affects you. This is the juncture where your conscious world joins the infinite knowing universe.

THE MEANING OF SUCCESS

Life doesn't ask you for great public accomplishments. Your love, your involvement in life, and your intention to do well are all that matter. That's the meaning of success. It's spiritual success. It's the success you take with you through eternity. And your reward is the comfort you feel in faith when love opens your heart to life's glories.

Think About It — Chapter 2

Thought #1:   As a new adult you're entering a time when you have to decide for yourself what your values are.

Thought #2:   Real security exists in being your own person. It's important to know when someone else's beliefs might be interfering with your own inner wisdom.

Thought #3:   If any old situation is good enough for you, that's exactly where you'll find yourself. Instead, let your values create your happiness.

Thought #4:   Know where you are and learn what you can to move you forward to where you want to be.

Thought #5:   Quality isn't having the biggest or the smallest. It's having enough of what's important. Completeness is found in your soul's fulfillment.

MONEY'S REAL VALUE IS THE
OPPORTUNITY IT GIVES YOU
TO HAVE WHAT'S IMPORTANT TO
YOUR LIFE.

WHAT YOU REQUIRE FROM LIFE
DEPENDS ON YOUR TASTES.
AND YOU'RE THE ONE
WHO CHOOSES THEM.

CHAPTER 3

MoNey

You probably already know that your most time-consuming effort will be your pursuit of money. In today's world money is your sustenance. It supports you and like the air you breathe gives you the promise of life. You'll think about it more than anything else. More than anything else you'll work to get it. And you'll spend a lot of time planning on how to get more. You'll have more feelings about it, good and bad, than any other experience you have. It's because your life depends on it.

Having enough money gives you a sense of security. On the other hand, feeling insufficient about money is stressful. It's well described in a scene from Charles Dickens' novel *David Copperfield*. In summary, the character Mr. Macawber says, "If you make twenty dollars a year and spend nineteen dollars, then life's happiness. But if you make twenty dollars a year and spend twenty-one, then life's misery." Having enough money is the difference between enjoying the freedom to control your own life—your most basic instinct—or obliging yourself to some debt that makes you a slave to financial circumstances decided by somebody else.

MONEY iS VALUE.

You trade money for things that support your life. It provides for your needs and pleasures. Money can be exchanged for just about anything—food, housing, communication services, clothing, transportation, and the power that cools your home and cooks your food. Your survival depends on money. It's important to have and there's nothing wrong with it. It's just cash, checks, and credit.

Exchanging money for goods and services is a great system. Purchases are all converted to a single unit of representative value. Its value is then determined by the changing value of those goods and services. And the trust that anyone has in money is in its ability to fairly represent their value over time.

Value can change for real or imagined reasons. The rarity of a product can make it more valuable because it's harder to get. And people will pay a higher price if they want it. On the other hand, a fashion going out of style could reduce its value because there's no desire for it. Then the price goes down to make it more attractive to a buyer. Values change and the value money represents changes with the times. The challenge is in agreeing to a value for money that fairly represents the goods and services traded for it.

You might meet people who tell you that you can't have money. They're wrong. There's nothing right or wrong about money in itself. It's paper. It's metal. It's an electronic tally. It's just something that represents value. Real value is in the things that money represents. The question isn't, "How much money do you have?" It's, "What are you going to buy?"

Money is a simple measurement to help us understand how we value life's details. It shows us the balance we have between our purpose and survival. Your right to live comes from God. It means that your right to have money is absolute. In today's society your sustenance is converted into monetary terms. So, money matters.

SUPPLY AND DEMAND

What someone gets for their money is decided by someone else's needs. So it's a question of who has the most opportunities. When the supply of something is plentiful, but demand for it is low, then the price paid for it will be low too. It's because those goods or services are easily available. So prices come down to increase their value to a buyer and add opportunities to the seller. Saving money is attractive to the buyer and creates demand for what's being sold. When the supply of something is scarce, but demand for it is high, then its price will be high too. Then competition for the limited resource increases its value and the price goes up. Prices rise or fall to increase sales or profits. And that means more money either for the buyer or the seller.

COMPETITION

Supply is subject to conditions and the first condition is competition. It depends on where else someone could go to meet their needs. There's nothing wrong with competition. If you have to compete then compete. It's not a matter of if you like it or not. Do your best and you'll get your share. People have different needs. And there are an equal number of people with a variety of ways to meet those needs. You'll decide, by the quality of your offer, the kind of business you'll find. And when you give good value you can expect good value in return.

You might not have to compete but you should always do your best. And it's not your best if you have to sacrifice your ideals to do it.

Your best is everything about you. So in your business life you should be the same person your soul's dream tells you to be. Do that and you'll never have to compete with anyone. They'll have to compete with you. Regardless of comparisons, you're in a one person race. Everyone's goals are different. What's important is to aim at your own target and not someone else's. A hit or a miss start at the same place.

SELFISHNESS

You have a right to live the life you choose. You have a right to have more money or more of whatever makes you happy. It's only wrong when it exists in the absence of love. Selfishness is an imbalance where a soul is dominated by the human part of its being. That human part demands life at any cost. But a human being is a balance between life and spirit.

It means respecting your opportunities without yielding to your body's insistent necessities. For example, relaxation is the rest you need but laziness is self-defeating. Your body's meant to empower your soul while it develops its role of leadership. Selfishness means losing that struggle for self-control. It denies faith. Rightfully and undeniably we're all self-centered. It's the familiarity we have with ourselves and our creative being. But a soul creates love in how it bonds with its nature. That's how conscious nature is meant to be used.

WEIGHING YOUR PRIORITIES

Money's real value is the opportunity it gives you to have what's important to your life. What you want depends on your personal tastes. So *you're* the one who makes the choices that give it meaning.

Having what you want doesn't have to be a hardship but it's often a challenge. And your plans will be more effective when you clearly understand what financial success means to you personally.

Would you be happier running a small grocery store or would you prefer working for a big corporation? Does being a TV star suit your plan or is a government job more desirable? When you come to terms with your financial success then you can cultivate what you need to make it happen. Focusing on yourself, you'll avoid wasting your time living someone else's values. What's right for you is yours to decide. So think about it.

Your comforts determine money's importance to you...and what you're willing to trade for it. Your priorities determine its value because it's measured in your time, effort, and peace of mind. So it's limited. Because it's limited, it shows you how you measure yourself. What you'll do for money is a measure of your intention. So it's your priorities that determine how financial success is important to your life.

Financial success and how it's judged is an important consideration in social circles. And you'll have to decide how important your success is in regard to these social pressures. But even where there's no social benefit there can be a psychological price. The cost of thoughtless ambition could be your happiness when ambition conflicts with your nature. Success is value on your own terms. So the benefit in improving your position in a social hierarchy is a personal matter.

WHERE DOES MONEY COME FROM?

Most likely it's not going to fall into your lap. You'll have to put it there yourself. Making money isn't a terrible dragon ready to devour you. It's a fact of life. And it's a factor whose nature should be understood to nurture and serve you.

So how do you get money? What can you trade for it? There's a popular concept that sees business cynically as "other people's money." But that's always the case. The money you want always belongs to somebody else. So how can you get them to give *you* their money? You do it by trading something of value for it—your time, skill, expertise, effort, or ideas. Or the goods and services they create.

The attitude "other people's money" means getting their money by any means possible, fair or not. It could mean extorting money by threatening someone with a problem or tricking them out of their money with a lie.

In contrast, the basic concept of business is that payment is an equal exchange of fair value. Fair means that all parties to the agreement know the price of what's traded and what's expected in return. And you can always make a good deal without compromising your responsibility to be honest.

GOOD QUALITY

Value depends on quality and the price you pay for it. And quality means different things to different people. The bottom line for everyone is achieving a balance between what they want and what it's worth to them. And the best quality will be how closely all your requirements are met.

When it's about your life, quality can be evaluated by how well your compromises fit your dreams. From that point of view, "best quality" is defined by what you've achieved in your choices. And best is always whatever satisfies your criteria for success. So your personal standards will always be the target for what quality means to you.

The best isn't always the biggest, the smallest, the most expensive, the cheapest, the prettiest, the most luxurious, the easiest, or the most technologically advanced. Though, in the right circumstances any of these could be best. A flawless diamond can be the most valuable regardless of its size. And a big diamond, while precious, might be too big for jewelry and is probably best in a museum where it can serve as a wonder for all to see. Size isn't the most important thing. Importance depends on the criteria for how something's used. Some diamonds are perfect for industry but useless as jewelry. And financial value doesn't always translate to emotional value. Sometimes best quality is just something you like. For whatever reason, it appeals to you.

Whatever quality is, you decide it. A Toyota Corolla might be the best quality car if your criteria are cost and reliability. Or a Chevrolet Corvette could be best if you're looking for speed, handling, and recognition. It's because your standards create a picture of quality framed in the details of your goals. And how well you meet your standards determines the value of everything for you.

You're always looking for the best return on your time and money. So specifically knowing what success means to you lets you trade for what you want without giving away more than you have to. That gives you the freedom to make a deal without missing opportunities when they show up. Your valuation of the circumstances—and knowing how the other party sees them—are important because you want to give them what they want as best you can. That's how you get closest to what you want.

Whatever a negotiation's about it depends on an agreement between you and someone else to determine the equal value that creates the fair exchange. The more you understand the effects of the agreement, the desires of the person you're trading with, and your own desires, the better chance you have for getting the most for what you offer.

GET YOUR MONEY'S WORTH

It's your responsibility to manage and protect your money. So it's important to watch it. Values can change but you still want to do your best in any deal. And it's in the details and opportunities, and thinking up creative alternatives, that you do that.

The greatest value of anything comes when you know what you want. And it's recognizing when it's yours. It means not getting more than what you want and paying for things you don't need. But it's just as important not to rationalize having less. When you do that you'll always feel you're missing something. So your decision to be clear on what you want is the most valuable decision you'll ever make.

Consider again purchasing a car. An automobile is transportation. At any price you'd want it to be reliable. And no matter how much money you have you wouldn't want to spend more than necessary to maintain it.

There are many cars that could satisfy your need to be able to go from one place to another. The advantages of a particular car can be great in quality but they all have the same basic concept. What everyone wants, more or less, is reliability, durability, utility, value, resale value, convenience, comfort, size, safety, styling, image, and the power to go fast or carry a heavy load.

Whatever you buy, the features you want relate to how you use it. And the qualities important to you are reflected in the price you're willing to pay for them. So knowing your satisfaction and being sure you have it are what's important. That's the best use for your money. Where's the value in a car that goes 150 miles an hour if you never drive that fast? What's the purpose in having a luxury car that costs $200,000 when you can get a similar car with the same features

GET YOUR MONEY'S WORTH *(continued)*

for $100,000? With everything practically equal, what do you really get for the extra money you're paying? Status? Maybe? And that's the most expensive thing you can buy because there's no price too high for it.

The same concept goes for whatever you buy. You'll always be comparing what you want to the wasted features you have to pay for. Everyone in business promotes what they're selling as the answer to your problems. And your friends and family can only advise you from their own point of view even though they want the best for you. So to be sure, trust yourself. You know what you want.

But you still have to be thoughtful. So you should seek guidance. You have to find information that confirms what you already know. And ask for suggestions. Then you can evaluate everything about your purchase. You'll know the full cost and exactly what you're getting in return. Using that knowledge you'll choose wisely and confidently. You'll get what you want and pay the right price for it. That's the value of money. And getting good value means you'll have more money to do other things that add richness to your life.

Making money consumes most of our time and effort. And including your time away from work, you'll often find yourself thinking about ways to make more money. It's because money means freedom and freedom is our natural security.

It's not a question of "earning money" where you're judged being worthy by yourself or someone else. Thinking that exposes you to the capricious concept that a justification other than price, quality, and competition decide how much money you should have. Your right to be prosperous is your birthright. It's given to you by God with God's approval. Everything else is negotiable.

GET SOME MONEY

Everyone wants to win the lottery. It's free money for a pittance of an investment. It's instant gratification and it could mean "instant freedom." At least it'll relieve you of a lot of life's problems. It means you won't have to work anymore at things you don't like. It could mean the end of your daily drudgery struggling for survival. And it could mean having everything you've ever wanted without any limits. It's like having your birthday every day.

We all want to feel secure and free from the concerns of having enough money or working too hard for it. We think that with winning the lottery we'll have unlimited resources. Well, right now, YOU are your unlimited resource. And every day there are opportunities waiting for you.

There are unlimited ways to make money. The methods are simple and easy to understand. The basic categories are: (1) get a job, (2) a career in sales, (3) go into business for yourself, (4) be a consultant, and (5) investing.

A JOB

There's always something to be traded. With a job you're paid for your time, effort, and expertise. You're paid for your ability to do something that solves someone's problem. And the importance of solving that problem determines what the solution's worth. How much you're paid is determined by the difficulty of the problem, the competition for the job, and more than anything else the increased value to someone for having their problem solved.

When you give good value for the money you're paid, when the situation's difficult, or when there's no one else to do the job, your work will be well rewarded. Personally you have a lot to offer. What you get in return is up to you. And it's up to you to communicate clearly what you expect as payment. The process of balancing these values is the meaning of negotiation.

Getting Paid

Depending on the job, employees are paid differently. A salaried employee is paid a fixed rate over a given period of time regardless of the hours they work or the work they do. Other employees receive an hourly wage for their work. Then your income depends on the number of hours you work per pay period, usually with your money paid weekly. By modern standards it means you're usually paid for working 40 hours per week. But under certain circumstances it can be figured differently.

An hourly wage creates the opportunity for you to make extra money working "overtime." Often the hours you work beyond the base 40-hour work week are paid at a premium rate where you receive "time and a half" or 1½ times your normal hourly rate for the extra hours you work.

And some service jobs have an opportunity for you to make "tips" paid directly to you by customers for the personal service you give them. That's in addition to your wages. Though, in some occupations the wages are lower in expectation of these tips.

More is expected of a salaried employee. And as a salaried worker it's common to work long hours without the satisfaction of extra pay to justify your efforts. However, the job usually comes with more responsibility, independence, and a bigger base paycheck. The freedom's offered because you're expected to get the job done without supervision. Your emotional bonus is the satisfaction that comes with doing things your own way without someone looking over your shoulder. It's the self-respect that comes with self-reliance. Salaried work can be more demanding but even without the additional pay it can reward you with a sense of accomplishment.

And salaried work has opportunities for performance bonuses, raises, and promotions with more responsibility and more pay. And the increased responsibility has the promise of more prestige and the added perks or extras given to dependable workers. A perk can be a company car, more vacation time, or the freedom to come and go as you please as long as your work's done. Perks make life easier. They're rewards for your accomplishments. And they're negotiable.

An hourly wage, on the other hand, is an exchange of your time for your employer's money. So your responsibilities and choices are limited. Then it's your job to complete assigned tasks. And your employer's responsibility is to pay you for the time you've worked. As a wage earner your responsibilities are finished when you punch out your time card at the end of the day. So there's less pressure on you to accomplish the company's overall goals. You're paid to complete tasks someone else decides lead to those goals.

As a wage earner you should be reliable. You should be at your workplace on time so your employer knows they can depend on you and plan accordingly. Your work should be done safely, both for you and your co-workers. And you should be alert to safety issues and speak up when you think a situation's unsafe. You should do your work efficiently and know what's needed to do your job properly without wasting time, effort, and materials. And it's vital to do your job well so, whatever the task, the result is dependable quality. So know what's expected of you and what "doing a good job" means to your employer. And get along with your co-workers because every product or service is a combined effort with everyone contributing to the result.

When you're paid by the hour great plans and strategies aren't expected of you. Reliability is. Reliability means being at work when your fellow workers expect your help. Reliability is your employer knowing they can count on you to do your job right. It means giving what's expected of you in return for what you're being paid to do.

With a smart employer, your pay should increase with your value as a dependable worker. But your commercial value has nothing to do with your value as a person. You'll always be priceless in God's plan. Your value in business, though, equals the contribution you make to someone who needs your help. Your value to an employer is determined by your job knowledge, work skills, and your ability to apply your knowledge and skills to solving work-related problems.

WHY DO YOU HAVE TO WORK?

Never see yourself as a victim of a job. Appreciate what you're doing and do your best at it. Find the value in it. That's your daily support. You can always look for a better job and do what you have to do to get it. At the end of the day your obligation is to yourself. That's the work ethic.

Work is a friend and shouldn't be avoided. Learn to embrace it. Work will give you everything you want in life. The skills and character values you learn working for someone else carry over to the work you do for yourself. So trust yourself and you'll be good at whatever you do.

Switching Jobs

You can increase your value by changing jobs. With the skills you learned in your current job you can leverage your abilities to get more pay at your next employer. And you can repeat this over and over. As you learn more you raise your value in the job market. And you can exploit this by putting gentle pressure on your employer to give you more money if they don't want to lose you to a competitor. Then with courtesy and respect, do what's best for you.

So never burn your bridges behind you. It's not unusual for a previous employer to hire you back and pay you good money for the new skills you bring with you. This is an effective method for advancement when you're just starting out making entry level pay. And it's a fast track method for learning your craft by exposing you to a cross section of experienced workers with many different skills. Your self-esteem will grow with your accomplishments and the realization that your co-workers don't consider you a trainee anymore. Then they'll respect the knowledge and skills you bring. And they'll appreciate being able to learn from you.

When you change jobs be responsible and respect that someone relied on you when you first accepted a job working for them. While it's your right to change jobs, and you should do it when it's in your best interests, it's still important to be fair. So be honest with your employer and give them the time they need to adjust to being without you.

The Paternal Work Relationship

In some situations you'll find yourself in a job where a paternal relationship's been established. The employer, acting like a parent, guides what's to be done and the family of workers does the work. This kind of relationship comes from the employees' respect for their boss's experience, commitment, and financial authority. And employers, who depend on their workers, can be equally protective of them. This reinforces the concept of a family where the boss represents a security figure as well as the authority for what's to be done.

As an employee thinking this way you might feel your efforts are part of your responsibility to please a loving parent. And where love and respect are present there's nothing wrong with it.

As an employee it's important to accept that it's your choice to be part of someone else's creation. It's a common choice and it has advantages. It's convenient and uncomplicated. It's simple knowing what's expected from you and your compensation. Best of all, once your day's over, the rest of your time is your own.

SPiRiTiNG ɊROUND EXERCiSE

Here are some questions to help you find jobs you might like. It's a lot about responsibility, what you like to do, and your lifestyle. And it's always about money.

- Do you like having responsibility?
- Do you want to be a leader?
- Do you mind taking orders?
- Do you like solving problems?
- Do you like physical work?
- Do you like to travel?
- Do the work hours matter?
- Do you want to work close to home?
- Do you want to make as much money as you can?
- Do you want to work in a specific industry?
- Do you have a preference for working in a factory, a store, an office, or outdoors?
- Do you like wearing a uniform?
- Do you like working by yourself or on a team?
- Do you like working with the public?

Your answers are a good start for comparing one job to another. But you're never limited to just one thing. And you never know what could develop from any job you take. While we don't always have the luxury of choosing everything we want about a job, you have a better chance of finding what you want when you know what you're looking for.

SELLiNG

On a basic level selling's a part of everyone's life. It's the fundamental question that supports everything that's traded. It's the offer to trade one thing for another.

Curiously, a sales job is seen in two different ways. If you're making money, it's considered respectable. But if you're not making money, it's considered lowly and contemptible, easy to do, and not very rewarding.

There are valid reasons for both views. The positive perspective is that your income depends on your efforts. When you're paid on commission, success or failure depends on what you produce. Even when an employer pays you by commission, a percentage of the sales you've made, it's ultimately the responsibility you have to yourself that decides your success. And it's possible to work hard and still be frustrated by a lack of sales and income. Because, in good times or bad, you always have to produce sales to make your commissions.

Selling is the only employment where you have the freedom to achieve a level of success you choose for yourself. The more you sell, the more you make. The secret is that success and income can be slow in the beginning. Getting established in sales takes time. And it takes time to learn how to sell. Like anything else, you have to learn the craft.

Keys to Sales Success

There are contributing factors to success in sales. Some factors you control and some you can't. A sale always depends on an agreement between you and your customer. And you can only guarantee your own half of the agreement. The necessary complement to your success is always someone else's decision. And while you can't control what someone's going to do, you can persist in making your presentation so attractive that they'll see the value in your offer, agree with you, and buy from you.

Resistance in selling comes from different places. It could be a lack of support from your employer. Then it's up to you to switch to a company that respects you and provides you with the help you need. Or it could be the product you're selling isn't desirable anymore. Then it's up to you to switch to selling a product that is desirable.

The craft of selling is in contacts and presentations. The more contacts you make, the more opportunities you'll have to present what you're selling. The more presentations you make, the more customers you'll find. And success comes from your customers. But it takes time to develop good relationships with enough customers to make money. Until you've established those relationships, sales may be slow and you can get anxious about having enough money to pay your bills—let alone have the success of your dreams.

In selling, the process of developing new relationships never ends. And it's how you respect your relationships that you create your reputation. A good reputation is a priceless commodity. And it's defined by your performance.

Starting Out Selling

Getting established in sales could take years while you develop your customer base. This is when it's important to improve your communication skills. As a good listener you'll learn how to understand your customer's needs. And when you satisfy their needs they'll be happy to pay you. They'll be grateful for you helping them. And when your customers trust your performance they'll come back for more. And they'll give you referrals so you can help their friends too. The beauty is how this process repeats itself to increase your sales and income.

Success in selling takes patience and persistence. And because it takes time you have to stay with it. So a career in selling needs survival training. You have to budget your money while you call on clients waiting for your income to begin. Or you'll have to find out where you can get financial support and have a plan to pay it back. It might be from a family member or a loan. A working spouse is helpful in bringing in the extra money needed to pay for life's necessities while you work at building up your client base. You might want to live with your parents or find a roommate to help cut expenses. When you choose a career in selling it's important to be prepared for the long haul and make your financial arrangements fit a picture where you might be on a tight budget for a while.

Then you have to train yourself to be a good salesperson. You have to develop the business knowledge and communication skills that give good service to your customers. You have to learn how to market yourself in the business community and present yourself well in one-on-one situations. Success in sales is cumulative. Your reputation's built on your successes. So it takes patience and effort to build a reputation that brings you repeat business, referrals, and more money.

Make Yourself Presentable

Having nice clothes and a good car is important to help you through this period. You'll be relying on both to make a good impression on your customers. Even without the strain of more expenses, money's tight when you're just starting out. Cars and clothes are expensive, especially if you don't have the money. But you can't put them off and still present a favorable impression in business. You'll have to find the money or borrow the clothes. You can always hide your old car around the corner and hope that your customers don't see it. It still has to be reliable though.

Your clothes and car are extensions of yourself and you're the first item to be sold. The car you drive and clothes you wear leave an impression of who you are and how you can be expected to perform. Your customers are going to make a choice about you. And they want to feel confident they can trust you to solve their problems. Simply put, they want their interests handled properly. As your customers' confidence grows they'll trust you to do more work for them. So they'll buy more of your products and services. And when you ask them to buy something from you they'll trust you and say yes. Then you'll make more sales and you'll make more money.

Salaried Selling or Working on a Draw

In addition to positions paying on commission, where it's the salesperson's job to create their own sales, there are salaried positions with regular paychecks unrelated to a person's sales. There the salesperson acts like a service person and the employer takes on the marketing responsibilities. Another option is to "get a draw." That's where an employer pays a draw ahead of the commissions they expect you to make. A draw is a modest payment, paid regularly, that helps reduce the financial pressure in the uncertainty of being paid on commission alone.

On commission, even in the best times your monthly income varies with your sales. And you're never sure how much money you'll make in any given week. A draw is money you can count on regardless of the commissions you've made. It provides you with stability so you can focus your attention on selling. The employer's thinking is that the salesperson will eventually produce more than enough to cover their draw. So everyone benefits. It's understood that some weeks are slower than others but with the benefit of a draw the salesperson can still pay their monthly bills.

The terms of a draw—the money, the pay period, how it's paid back if it's repaid, and how long it continues—are decided by an agreement between you and your employer. It's determined by the arrangement you negotiate. And it can be as varied as any agreement that serves the particular needs of the parties involved. Anyway, your goal is to exceed your draw. You should only count on a draw to cover your expenses at the start of your sales career.

AGREEMENTS

It's important to know the details of your agreements so everyone's responsibilities are understood. It'll go a long way to defusing disagreements which may occur in the future. It's your right to know the terms of your agreements. It's a necessity to the financial responsibility you owe to yourself.

There's nothing wrong in asking for what you want and negotiating your best deal possible. Ask courteously and you deserve to be treated the same. If you aren't treated respectfully, it's a warning flag to be cautious in your dealings with the other person. Always give yourself the benefit of the doubt. Use good judgment. And you'll do fine.

In any conflict over an agreement everyone's going to protect themselves first. Just be aware that situations change. Where you see potential for a change you can be prepared with a response as part of your plan. A simple agreement in writing is the best protection for everyone. It's not always possible because in every agreement there's an element of trust to be respected. You can try for it though. If it's not possible, keep your records and correspondence put safely away. You can depend on those files to clarify the details after everyone's forgotten the original agreement. You can always throw them out later.

THE PERKS

You'll find extraordinary perks in a sales career. The confidence you need in selling is put to good use in every part of your life. So you learn to trust your abilities. Believing in yourself is your belief in your offer. And the confidence you show in yourself is the same confidence your customers will have in you. It's in this trust that you create harmony with your customers. Your customers will believe that what you tell them is true. But you don't need complete confidence to start. Self-confidence is something you can learn. All you need is the intention to do well, the desire to work out problems, and your decision to be a confident person.

Other perks include the real friendships you build with your customers. The trust you share in your business responsibilities is easily carried over to your personal relationship especially where you have common interests. These can be mature lasting friendships based on honesty and support. A real friend is a priceless resource. And working together and depending on someone to solve a business problem is a great way to test a friendship.

A big motivation in selling is service. You have the satisfaction of helping somebody solve their problem. A salesperson should be dedicated to satisfying their customers' needs. In sales your pay is based on how well you help someone else. When you help someone have what they want and they feel good about it they're better off. You've provided good value and you should be paid for it. Your greatest asset will be how well you understand your customers' desires beyond the actual goods and services you sell. What's important is what the sale means to your customer in personal terms. How it fits their goals. It could mean more money, a promotion, or less work.

Whatever it is, their personal desires are as important to the sale as any benefit of your product or service might be. That's the real way to help your customers.

In most sales jobs you have the independence that comes with self-reliance. And you'll be able to enjoy your accomplishments without all the work that comes with running a business.

A Job or a Joke?

Then why's selling still considered a joke? Why is it thought of as a job of last resort? Still, every product or service is sold by someone to someone else. From glow-in-the-dark backscratchers to penicillin, from jelly beans to car insurance, and from space stations to skateboards, there's selling going on as part of the commercial process. Selling's important because it demonstrates the benefits of one thing over another or the benefit of having something compared to being without it. The joke is that you have to make sales to make money. But it's more than a joke. It's the challenge to be successful.

Selling is a genuine service when it's done with your customers' interests in mind. You provide the knowledge of what to expect and how to do it right. So you're trading your ability to solve problems. And in life's reciprocal process you should expect your fair share in return.

The foundation of an offer is its truthfulness. It's your honest presentation of the facts as you understand them. When you present your offer so your customer has the necessary details, they can decide for themselves what's best for them. Then you're doing your job. When you do that you'll always have plenty of customers wanting to work with you. If you place yourself above your customers' interests, if you're dishonest, or if you withhold information to mislead a customer, you'll eventually find that anyone who knows you won't buy from you. And you'll be left with the limited market and limited

SPiRiTiNG AROUND EXERCiSE

Selling has a potential not available in other jobs. It's the freedom to be your own boss without having to handle the endless problems of ownership. And you can make just as much money when you're successful at it. The essential element in selling is getting along with people you don't know yet. And developing trust with them. That's the challenge. It can be very rewarding if you're suited to it. If you like people, you can learn how to sell to them. And you can start by asking yourself some questions.

- Are you self-reliant?
- Do you like a personal challenge?
- Can you accept criticism without taking it personally?
- Can you shrug off defeat, learn from your mistakes, and do better the next time?
- Do you like solving problems?
- Are you comfortable talking to people or would you like to learn how?
- Can you dedicate yourself to learning about the product you're selling?
- Can you dedicate yourself to learning the craft of selling?
- Do you have the patience to do the work of selling?
- Are you financially ambitious?
- Are you interested in human psychology and behavior?
- Are you honest?
- Do you see the benefit in everyone getting what they want in a relationship?
- Can you see selling as a service?

These questions give some insight into the mind of a salesperson. Selling might be perfect for you. Like anything else, you're successful when you work at it. Selling's unique benefit is that, besides your income, it gives you life skills that you use every day.

income that comes from people who you'll only fool once. Reputation goes two ways. Your reputation can be a rewarding asset if you respect it and a forbidding obstacle when you ignore it.

Selling's a funny kind of job where you're always working, you're always off, and you're always looking for new opportunities. So if you want to be successful in sales, get on the phone and make an offer.

YOUR OWN BUSINESS

Another way to make money, closely related to selling, is being in business for yourself. That's because sales are the lifeblood of any business. *Sales are business.* Selling creates the agreement that starts the business relationship and the arrangement for trading your goods and services for your customers' money.

With a business you create a mechanism for creating income. You could invent something or provide a service that supports the new technologies. Or you could open a pizza restaurant and build on proven successes that serve well known needs. There's always room for another pizza parlor.

Still, building a business can be hard. There's a lot to do and it's very demanding. It can mean hiring help, borrowing money, and working long hours. When you start a business you have to be ready to make a commitment with everything you have. Developing a business takes time and money. And more likely than not, it'll take more than you have. Creating resources is a constant fact of business.

Here are some broad categories that cover the many tasks it takes to run a successful business.

In all, there are hundreds of details you'll have to attend to if you want to be successful. Everything won't need your attention

ASPECTS OF RUNNING A SUCCESSFUL BUSINESS

- Outstanding Marketing
- Convincing Advertising
- Productive Selling
- Quality Customer Service
- Effective Products and Services
- Practical Facility Management
- Timely Inventory Control
- Careful Accounting
- Sensible Borrowing
- Reasonable Negotiations
- Up to Date Collections
- Orderly Record Management
- Anticipated Taxes and Insurance
- Enlightened Employee Relations
- Considered Legal Responsibilities
- Correctly Qualifying Credit Worthiness
- Constant Concern for Controlling Costs
- Careful Maintenance of High Standards of Performance

constantly but it might seem like it does. Something's always happening. And there's always something more you can do to improve your business.

Of course, the only criterion for success in business is to be profitable. Your best intentions may be admirable but without profits to pay your bills it'll be a short-lived endeavor. You'll be investing a large part of yourself in your quest for financial freedom. Don't waste it. Think long-term. Think profits.

PROFiT iN A SPiRiTUAL SENSE

Whatever form your business takes, you're trading something for something else. Your goal is to create more money than you started with, *your profits*. But there are two ways to look at it.

From one perspective you can choose a mercenary attitude where all you want is to get as much money as you can and give as little as possible in return. Pursuing business that way, you'd do anything, say anything, and promise anything if you thought it could increase your profits. Again, it's the interpretation of business as "other people's money." It sees business as separate from spirit. And it's a frightened outlook on survival.

A more prosperous attitude is to focus on fairness and providing good value to your customers. You can serve your customers' needs and make money at it. Let that be your mission statement. In return, you can expect a good life for yourself. It's your faith in fairness that respects your spiritual responsibility in business. To honor yourself in business, be clear what your customers want and give it to them. But remember, the consideration you give to your customers must balance equally with your own expectations.

Business People Need Help Too.

You can run a business by yourself or you can consider splitting the responsibilities with a *partner*. In a partnership everyone draws on the strengths of each partner including the money they bring to the venture. The benefit of working with partners is that you can divide the tasks according to who does what the best and where each partner can make the greatest contribution.

Or you might hire *employees* to do the work for you. You can hire people full-time, part-time, or for special projects as you need them. And you can "outsource" or "contract" other companies to do specific jobs for you. For example, you might use an accountant to do your bookkeeping and taxes so you can spend your time where it's more important to growing your business. So you have to decide where your best interests are when you compare the benefit of hiring an outside service to the cost of paying for it. And remember that employees come with employer responsibilities. There are government regulations and extra costs like workman's compensation and unemployment insurance to consider.

So it's important to seek expert advice before you make your financial commitment. A business is a big responsibility. So to insure your success you should know what to expect and the costs involved. Or you may be trapped by unexpected regulations, taxes, and the rising costs of doing business. Being unprepared for expenses can sink your business before you've even started. Money is the strength of your business. It empowers your business to grow. And it sustains your business while you work at getting more revenue. Knowing your costs lets you plan for them. It's the power in your budget.

Your Own Business: A Worthy Challenge

Being in business can be both financially and emotionally rewarding. In a successful business the pressure's on you to solve your problems creatively instead of just throwing money at them. It tests you. But if you like a challenge, that's the charm of it.

Best of all, with your own business you have no limits. You can create the business that fits your needs, not someone else's. Your business can be structured to suit *you*. You can create something to fit your lifestyle or follow a more traditional model. You'll decide the hours you'll work, the places you'll be, and what you'll do there. Just turn a profit. If you're not making money you'll have to change your plan.

Your business can give you financial freedom and the satisfaction that comes with creating something you've designed for yourself. At the same time it can make endless demands on your time and energy. But in business the problems you face are the ones that you've chosen. And the glory in your success is a gift to you from God.

There are all types of businesses and you can be successful at any of them. Each has its own advantages and disadvantages. How you judge the value of a particular business is up to you. You could buy a franchise, start something new, or invent something and license it to someone else to sell. You can sell wholesale to other companies or retail to the public. You can manufacture a product or provide a service. You can serve the world or be a local business in your neighborhood. The particulars don't matter because every business is about trade. It's only important to make a profit on what you're trading. And it's an honorable way to make money.

CONSULTiNG

Another way to make money is to be a consultant. It's a slightly different business structure. As a consultant your knowledge and communication skills are your product. A consultant is an independent problem-solver. So a consultant needs the experience to identify problems and the ability to present alternative solutions.

Different plans have different costs and solve problems in different ways with different features and different results. The consultant's job is to present the available options that could help their employer. Then the employer has to make their own decision on what to do.

An Open Field

There's no age requirement for consulting work. This is shown in the explosion of opportunity for young people in the computer industry. So much is new to everyone. And a young person has just as much opportunity as someone older if they're willing to invest their time in learning the new technology. It's all easy if you know how to do it.

Remember, as a new adult you don't have a career yet. You're the proverbial blank slate, unencumbered by the weight of life's responsibilities. With clear goals, hard work, and dedication, you can be an expert in any field you choose. And any subject you study and understand creates an opportunity for you to market your knowledge.

Consulting Pays

When you're paid to use your knowledge on a case-by-case basis and suggest solutions to problems, you're a consultant. You're paid for what you know but not like an instructor who's paid to teach what they know. As a consultant you're employed to solve someone's specific problem. And it could range from suggesting methods for more efficient production to how to remove birds from an airport runway.

Once problems are identified and solutions presented the consultant's job is done. Being a consultant is a temporary position. It only requires the limited term of the employment contract. It could be for a day or a year. Or it could mean making yourself available at a moment's notice to be consulted whenever a related problem arises. Whatever your agreement, you succeed by creating ways for your employer to improve their business or by providing connections to other business people who can help your employer.

Like any enterprise, you need customers for your consulting business. But you'll be well paid for your profit-building ideas when your suggestions are successful. And as the word gets around, your business will grow.

Knowledge Is Money.

So how does someone become a consultant? Well, first you exploit yourself. You exploit your interests and your talents. You do more of what you like doing the best. You read more about the subjects you enjoy the most. And you think a lot about things that give you a sense of accomplishment.

And you'll associate with knowledgeable people who share your expertise. People with common interests enjoy each other's company and share in the enthusiasm for their chosen field. So you'll find friendships.

No matter what your age, your love for your subject will entitle you to be called a "colleague." So explore your subject. Look for it everywhere. Evaluate past studies in the light of new discoveries. And when you read the professional journals you'll have the most advanced research available to the general community. You'll have more knowledge than many experienced professionals just because they haven't had time to keep up with the latest developments. Add some confidence and you're a consultant!

Selling Solutions

Once you're a consultant, you'll be well paid for the hours you invested in understanding your subject. People have problems that your knowledge can solve. And they'll gladly pay you for that knowledge rather than investing the time to learn as much as you already know. Then it's a simple matter to market yourself and make people aware that you can help them.

The knowledge you offer can be about anything; computers, animal training, or any topic with a need for it and the potential to do business. Your interests are your only boundaries. And by exploiting your interests you're doing something you love. It's something you can often do on your own schedule too. And if you ever leave consulting work, your knowledge makes you more marketable when you look for a job.

SPIRITING AROUND EXERCISE

Ask yourself if there's anything you love doing so much that someone would pay to learn about it from you. Or is there something you've been doing for so long that you could easily teach it to someone else? And get paid for it.

BE AN INVESTOR.

Another way to make money is by investing. It can be as personal as investing in a friend's business. Or you can invest in the worldwide financial markets with names like The New York Stock Exchange, NASDAQ, or The Chicago Board of Trade where stocks, bonds, commodities, and a variety of financial instruments are traded every day. But even with the largest multi-national corporations it's still the simple concept of buying something and hoping to make a profit when the value of it goes up.

Investing in a Private Business

Especially when investing with friends, it's important to have a clearly defined written agreement that explains what you're getting for your money. You should know ahead of time how your principal—the amount of money you've invested—will be returned to you as well as how you're paid your share of the profits or your interest on a loan. **A financially responsible person knows the terms of their investment.**

Here are some things to consider as an investor. And knowing these details can help you decide if a particular investment is the best use for your money.

- Is your investment considered a loan to be paid back over a fixed period of time with interest or are you buying part of a business where you're sharing the risks and opportunities of ownership?

- What's the rate of return—your gross profit expressed as a percentage—going to be? What's it in dollars?

- How often will you receive payments?

- When will your investment be paid back completely?

- What insurance do you have that your investment's secure?

- Can you sell your investment to somebody else?

- What rights will you have in voicing your opinion about how the business is run or how your investment's protected?

- How does it compare to a different investment you could make with your money?

Keep in mind that businesses can fail. They can go out of business and take your investment with them. It can be incompetent management or changing market conditions that cause a company to fail. Competition can force costs up or prices down. Or industry innovations can make a company's services obsolete and unmarketable. It all means that under certain conditions you can lose your investment. Forget about the profits; you could lose *all* your money.

The Market

Besides investing with someone you know, you can own shares of companies traded in the stock markets. In the markets you have an opportunity to invest in the largest corporations in America as well as those in other countries. By buying stocks you become a corporate shareholder, a part owner in that company. The proportion of your investment may be small in relation to the value of the company but you benefit as much as anyone else

MY BROKER

Working with a good stockbroker is helpful. Their normal workday is buying and selling stocks for their clients. They have training, experience, information, and insight into the ups and downs of the markets. Hopefully they know what makes the markets react and which stocks are positioned to go up or down. You can learn a lot about investing just by talking to them, asking questions, and listening to their point of view. With the right knowledge, temperament, and attention to what you're doing, you can own stocks for a profit.

You should realize that stockbrokers make money by handling your transactions. The more trades you make, the more money they make. But they'll share their knowledge with you as part of their service. They want you to make money. They want you to use their services and come back to do more trades. But keep in mind that when they're paid on commission it's in their interests to have you buying and selling stocks.

when the price of your shares goes higher than what you paid for them. Then you can sell your shares for a profit. But your shares can also go down if other investors lack an interest in owning them. The price of stocks, bonds, and other financial tools go up or down depending on their desirability in the markets.

It's individual investors —like you—and large institutional investors—like pension and mutual funds—who bid for stocks depending on their anticipated value. The premise is that people will buy a stock or any financial instrument they believe is going higher to increase the value of their investment. The number of shares you own and the price you paid for them stays the same but the value of your investment increases as its price rises in the marketplace. Then if you want you can sell your shares and take your money. The money you've made—the difference between what you paid for a stock and what you sold it at—is your profit.

Remember, stocks go down too. And you lose money when the price of your stock falls to less than what you paid for it. So it's important to be knowledgeable about your investments if you want to make money. There's no guarantee you'll make money. There are too many variables beyond your control. But at least you can learn to be a smart investor.

A Risk You Can't Control

You can take a risk and buy a stock but you can't control where it's going. So to protect yourself when you invest in stocks you should be an informed consumer. It helps to talk to other investors and see what you can learn. You can join an investment club or start one of your own. In a club atmosphere you benefit from sharing ideas and experience with other investors without the influence of someone trying to do business with you.

In addition you should learn where stockbrokers go for their information. Find out who are the most respected advisors in the investment industry. Ask your stockbroker which books they recommend. Ask them which publications and financial shows they like. And where on the Internet they go for research.

There are different strategies for investing. You can learn them and be successful as long as you pay attention to what you're doing. But even careful planning can't predict when markets will move dramatically for unexpected reasons. So you should know ahead of time the moves you'll make when a change in market conditions affects your investments. Then you can act quickly to take advantage of your preparation or wait patiently till the next change brings you a new opportunity.

It's possible to make money in the stock market. But to be successful you have to invest wisely. Wise investing includes researching the internal strengths and weaknesses of individual stocks, paying attention to corporate performance, and knowing what affects stock market moves. Then you can adjust your portfolio to changing market conditions, protect your investments, and keep your returns high. There's always a risk you could lose your money but the historic trend is that owning stocks has profited most people in the long run.

Where people live in a secure environment, investors feel safe and businesses and stocks should do well. A growing economy adds flexibility to investing. You can trade your stocks daily, taking profits as you can, or invest long term and watch the value of your stocks grow steadily over time. Whatever your financial objectives may be, your best friends in investing will always be your education, planning, and vigilance. Then, whatever happens you can respond to it sensibly.

If you don't prepare yourself and keep an eye on your money, your investments will be little more than a wild gamble with your path dimly lit by some Wall Street loudmouth who's just luckier than most. That might be okay for them but it may not turn out so well for you. Worse yet is to find yourself leaning on advice from some salesperson who isn't being honest about the risk or return of some investment they want you to buy. You can fall into the trap of easy greed and lose your money when you believe someone's puffed-up stories instead of trusting your own research.

Whatever you do, don't trust one person for all the answers. Someone with the best intentions could have wrong information. And investing is all about being informed. When your investments go up and you make money you'll be happy. When your investments go down and you lose money you'll be unhappy. So as an investor you're always trying to figure out the best thing to do in a changing world. Many things affect the world's economies and their financial markets. But most important of all is society's confidence in its future.

Keep in Mind

Investing is easy to do but it's not simple. Besides commissions to pay, there could be management fees and tax liabilities. You'll be in a business relationship so you have to know your responsibilities. And you can learn all you can or at least enough to be a successful investor. Most important is that it's up to you to watch your money. Your money is the tool you use to make investments. So take care of it.

In addition to your shares going up there are other ways to make money owning stocks. Some stocks pay a dividend, your portion of the company's earnings when they're paid out to stockholders. Or you could benefit from a merger or acquisition where two companies join together to save on costs and increase their marketability. This can drive up the price of your shares when other investors anticipate their increased value and want to buy your stock. Also a stock can split. This increases the number of shares you own without you investing more money, though the price of each share is lower to maintain the original value of your investment. While mainly a marketing tool, it still indicates growth. Its appeal is that it increases the value of your investment when your stock's price rises and you now own more shares.

And human creativity is always devising new ways to invest. But new investment instruments have unproven track records. They can promise big returns but the profits may depend on unreliable expectations. So you should examine every investment mechanism carefully. As always, you have to be on guard to reduce your risks and protect your investment.

Other Markets

There are other established markets where you can put your money to work for you. Commodities, interest rate futures, options, metals, currencies, and real estate all offer appreciation opportunities. And there are bond markets where you'll find a variety of financial vehicles that do well and can balance your portfolio. There are also active markets in art and collectibles that give you the opportunity to invest in things you like. And they've shown to appreciate over time. But there are risks to consider. And you'll find advantages and disadvantages in any investment you choose. So learn what they are, see how they affect you, and decide which investments meet your goals.

SPIRITING AROUND EXERCISE

Investing is a little like gambling because you never know just what's going to happen. You don't control it. An investor can try to be educated but stocks don't always move in the direction of common sense. Too often the experts come out and tell us why something happened yesterday and not what's going to happen tomorrow. So if you want to be an investor here are some questions to ask.

- Can you afford to lose the money you've invested?
- Are you willing to watch your investments?
- Are you willing to learn the strategies and tactics of investing?
- Do you understand the factors that affect an investment?
- Have you explored different ways to invest your money?
- Have you decided which ones suit your needs?
- Do you have the patience to stick with your investments?
- Are you ready to act and take advantage of an opportunity?
- Do you have the temperament to weather market fluctuations?
- Do you have the time to research your investments?
- Will you rely on someone else to do it?
- Do you think other investors are smarter than you?
- Do you believe everything people tell you?
- Are you looking for a big score?
- Do you realize that investing is about human behavior as much as economics?

When you have money you don't need to live on you can put it to work for you to make more money. Whether you invest safely in a government guaranteed savings account or wildly in some harebrained scheme, it depends on your caution and common sense to make the most of it.

CREDIT, BUDGETS, AND COMMON SENSE

However you make money, how much you have depends on how you manage it. Management is having goals and plans to reach them. It's managing your resources and opportunities. That's a long-term responsibility. And your future starts tomorrow, not twenty years from now. How you use money follows you through life because it marks your choices. And that includes the money you borrow.

Having good credit is expected but bad credit can be a warning sign of bad judgment. Even when forces beyond your control create financial problems for you, people will still want the money you owe them. Whether it's a friend or a business, they trusted you when you agreed to pay them.

Bad credit is a social problem. It's more than just disrespect for your agreements. It's a lack of respect for fairness. And that's important to everyone. Even when a desperate financial situation makes paying back a debt impossible, you should never dismiss your responsibility. Your intention should always be to pay what you owe. Even if you need more time than you originally planned for. You owe that to yourself.

Though you can use it any way you want, credit's just a rental. You're renting the use of the money and fees are attached. It's not free. It has to be paid back. But it's an opportunity to create a productive budget by using that money to make a better life for yourself. A budget balances your income with your expenses according to your priorities. So how you spend your money indicates your values.

THE TAXES

Your income is subject to taxes so you should make an effort to know the tax laws that affect you. And the laws change so you have to keep up with them. As part of your financial plan it's important to consider your taxes. It's a real expense. And respecting your liabilities is a mature attitude towards handling your money. So you should bring up the question of taxes in every financial decision to know its real cost.

You should get professional advice on matters concerning your money and the law. While lawyers and accountants are expensive, they're insurance against future problems. And in the long run that can save you time, money, and a lot of aggravation.

Taxes aren't bad. They're a miracle of civilization. We pay a small part of the money we have so we can share the benefits of a community. Your taxes pay for public roads, public schools, and the entire spectrum of civil service management that keeps our social system secure and productive. Taxes are the way a community shares expenses. Taxes create the resources that give a community the opportunity to have things that everyone can use.

No one minds paying their fair share. What we hate is finding self-serving people using the tax system to their own advantage without considering the rest of us. There are honest people in government who still have different ideas on who pays taxes and how to spend the money. Your responsibility is to choose those people. Your representation affects your finances. They're your voice on how your money is spent. So vote for them if you want to have a say in the matter.

The challenge is how the government manages our money. Wasting tax revenues is everyone's loss. Where there's mismanagement or corruption, it takes from everyone. With taxes, consideration for the majority, respect for the minority, and attentiveness to the needs of every individual are all needed to maintain a community's integrity.

Good government is designed to be fair. And it recognizes that things in a community change. That includes the demographics of the people who live there. And while the concept of fairness stays the same, the meaning of "what's fair" to a community's new incarnations should be continually revised. So with a community's maturing wisdom the debate on fairness must continue.

Fairness keeps responsibilities equal. But the equation needs constant attention if everyone's going to do well. So it takes faith to give up what you think you need for the sake of your community. Fairness is the spiritual guide to prosperity because it trusts that love supports us. And that's the key to being a complete person…successful in life and spirit.

THE ROAD TO RICHES

You'll always need more money. Your need for money is continuous because life is a material process. Humanity is a system designed to succeed in its environment. And today the fuel you need to energize this sophisticated system is money.

The cost of living is always high. A thousand years ago people complained about the high cost of living and a thousand years from now we'll still moan about it. Because people will always push the limits of what they think they can get in trade. But you'll find that a comfortable life is usually available at reasonable prices.

How you value money equals the quality of life you want. And there's no one path that's superior to all others. The important criterion is that you have what you want and not just what you can afford at the moment. Free time might be more important to you than having a fancy car. And there are many principles of conscience that are more expensive than any object you can own. It's up to you to decide the values of your life. No one else should do that for you. If you're undecided what to do, just choose to continue on some useful path till you do know. You have no debts anywhere other than to your own heart's desire. And it's in your heart that you connect to God's plan for you. That's where you'll find your harmony with life.

THiNK ABOUT iT — CHAPTER 3

THOUGHT #1: *Having enough money is the difference between controlling your own life and obliging yourself to some responsibility that makes you a slave to financial circumstances decided by somebody else.*

THOUGHT #2: *There's nothing wrong with money. It's just something to represent value. That's all it is.*

THOUGHT #3: *Your plan for the future is most effective when you understand what financial success means to you personally.*

THOUGHT #4: *Find the approach to making money that fits you— working for someone else, selling, having your own business, consulting, or investing. And be flexible. You're growing and your work life evolves.*

THOUGHT #5: *We all think winning the lottery means we'll have unlimited resources. Well, right now, YOU are your own unlimited resource. Every day you have skills and talents, and the opportunities they create. But it takes action on your part to direct them.*

To be balanced you must
be conscious
That love affects you.

So you should be as fair
to yourself as you are to
anyone else

And understand that everyone
has their own needs and
limitations.
And that through it all,
love supports us.

CHAPTER 4

Love

Love. Make love. Puppy love. In love. Do it for love. Take a lover. Sex. Romance. Pick-up. Gay. Lesbian. Queer. Masturbate. Flirt. Knocked up. Having a baby. Spin the bottle. Dumped.

Whoa now! That's way too fast! But we're just starting to look at love, sex, and relationships and how we interpret our reproductive nature...our inescapable sexuality.

The birds and the bees. Striptease. Sex education. Affection. Erection. Dating. Making out. Going steady. Breaking up. An item. A crush. Engaged. Divorced. Annulled. Wham, bam, thank you ma'am. All's fair in love and war. Lust. Turn on. Hot. Wet. Hard. Horny. Hump. Fellatio. Blow job. Vows. Coming. I love you. I can't live without you. Girlfriend. Tomboy. Boy toy. Sugar daddy. Bosom. Bust. Tits. Knockers. Cans. Cleavage. Falsies. Boob job. Pussy. Vaginal. G-spot. Cunnilingus. Erotic. Sperm. Dick. Prick. Balls. Penis.

Suck it. Eat me. Kiss. Cuddle. Bride. Groom. Honeymoon. Cuckold. Commitment. I've never been happier. Contraceptive. The Pill. Condom. Diaphragm. Nonoxynol-9. RU486. KY Jelly. Safe sex. Blind date. Ruffies. Made for each other. Knight in shining armor. Fluffer. Voyeur. Chastity belt. Good girl. Gold digger. Gigolo. Waiting for the right one. Soul mate. Foreplay. Fall in love. Harem. Eunuch. Ask her out. True love. Player. *Sex in the City. The Bachelor. The Love Connection.* Sex addict. Tantric. Having an affair. Cheating. STDs. Herpes. Crabs. Syphilis. The clap. Gonorrhea. AIDS. Protection. Virgin. Don Juan. Casanova. Mata Hari. Celibate. Abstinent. Red light district. Madly in love. Missionary position. Phallic. Prurient. Obscene. XXX. Doggy style. Love, honor, and obey. Boner. Dildo. Vibrator. S&M. Hooker. Fetish. Porno. Dating service. Phone sex. Carnal knowledge. Orgasm. Get laid. Penetration. Slut. Whore. He likes you. She's crazy about him. Sex life. Forever.

Even with a short list you still get the picture. Love and sex are mysteries full of pain and joy. And they have different meanings for each of us. So how do we explain them? We want love and sex as part of our lives but we're afraid of them too. So how do we honor our sexuality as a part of ourselves? Sex is the continuity of life so it's compelling. It drives us to crave agreement with willing partners but it's filled with complex responsibilities.

Confusion about sex and romance is a burdensome distraction. Desire can be hard to control as it weaves itself through your consciousness. It's always on our minds, just below the surface, and there are a lot of opinions on it. And that means conflicting ideas for young minds to consider. All you have to know is that if you're honest with yourself, accept your sexuality, and take the time to think about it; it'll eventually make sense to you.

EVOLViNG SEXUʀLiTy

It takes time and experience to see sex in its entirety. Nations and generations have had vastly different attitudes towards it. For the answers to many of your questions you'll need your own experience to understand the facts about which so many public judgments are made. Then the commentaries and criticisms can wait while you form your own opinion on the meaning of sex. One you'll respect and enjoy. To avoid the pitfalls that can affect your sexual experience—sexually transmitted diseases, unwanted pregnancies, and disappointing relationships, your best protection will always be getting good advice and having the patience to learn about your own sexuality—one of the most complex responsibilities in life.

Sex can take a lifetime to learn and you grow with it. We usually see our sexual experience from a limited perspective when we're young but from a wiser perspective as we grow older. And it gets easier as time matures us. Conflicts get ironed out. Questions get answered. It's still a negotiation but it's not an unknown anymore. This should help you be patient as you become a sexually responsible person. Sex presents resistance in life because it isn't your choice alone. It needs agreement to complete itself. But it's naturally attractive to both partners. And with agreement you can responsibly satisfy your sex drive.

Sexual relationships are among the most intense personal relationships you can have. It physically brings people together with the promise of life's continuity. Sex is the bridge to humanity's existence. And it perpetuates the physical love we represent in our humanity. Sex manifests that love.

Lovemaking's a twin with emotional love and both are siblings to spiritual love. In spiritual love is love for your family, love for yourself, love for your friends, love for your country, love for humanity, love for life, and love for God. And it means more than just giving your love. It's how you receive love as well.

HOW DO WE LOVE?

Where's the justice with love? Even with the endless variety of personalities, with all their plans and preferences, there's still a simple guide to understanding love. It's in the Bible, 1 Corinthians 13. And it relates to everyone equally.

> *Love is patient. Love is kind. Love envies no one. Love is never boastful, nor conceited, nor rude. Never selfish nor quick to take offense.*

> *Love keeps no score of wrongs, does not gloat over another's sins, but delights in truth. There is nothing love cannot face; there is no limit to its faith, its hope, and its endurance.*

> *In a word, there are three things that last forever; Faith, Hope, and Love, but the greatest of them all is LOVE.*

It's how we apply this wisdom that's the hard part. It's the part that we have to work on to be successful. It's the part about loving. Love's the stuff of the universe. It's the measure of life's existence. Simply put, it's important and it matters. And it matters *more than anything else.*

We live in a practical world where forces press on us from without, from within, and from mysterious places deep in our consciousness. So to achieve balance you have to be conscious that love affects you.

So be as fair to yourself as you are to anyone else and understand that everyone has needs, desires, and limitations. And that still through it all love supports us. Love forces us into balance with God's plan by stretching us to be more of who we are as human beings.

DISCOVERING WHAT MATTERS

The strongest forces in our lives are within us. Psychically we're drawn to each other. The old joke is that the primal force bringing people together is sex but the real power between people is *communication.* Communication is the reunification of what's been individualized through God's creation. Now we're all trying to combine with each other back into the conscious wholeness of God. The inventions that have always had the greatest impact on humanity had to do with bringing people together and helping them communicate. From forest trails to bullet trains and from sign language to the Internet we've continually explored ways to reassemble. The human desire to join together is as natural as saying "hello."

So what does it mean to a young person who's trying to figure out what life has to offer and what they can give back in return? Instead of establishing a different philosophy for every relationship there's a root sensibility from where all of your thoughts on love can grow. The emotional intensity or the importance you put on a relationship is different for everyone. And as you examine yourself through your relationships you'll discover that *it's caring that matters.* How you act on how you care is the challenge.

Anytime you're interacting with others the road can be frustrating. A relationship means you have to consider what someone else wants in relation to your own sense of harmony. You might not want to be with someone who wants to be with you. Or someone you like may not like you. Even when people care about each other their feelings can be different on whether they're friends, lovers, or lifetime partners. This all has to be considered. A relationship shouldn't be discarded just because it doesn't match the picture you've imagined. A relationship should be appreciated and embraced for its reality and the manifestation of love it presents—whatever it is.

BEYOND THE FAMILY

Your family is your foundation and starting point for your experience with love. A loving family can be the support system you need for life's adventure. On the other hand, a dysfunctional family can sour your attitude towards life. Whether your family is wise and well-intentioned or jealous and hateful, you still have to learn to make the best of it. Even at a young age your life and what you accomplish is up to you.

Good or bad, your upbringing is rich with potential and opportunities for you. And don't think that things have to be a certain way or match an idyllic representation of some sitcom writer's fiction. Even at its best, a family means different things to each of us. Whatever it is, your family is the start of your education. Your job is to apply what you learn and make your life better.

You have to use your natural abilities and God-given common sense to make the decision to be a happy person. Your lack of experience and society's pressures can make it seem like it's harder than it has to be. But that's the way life is. What you can do is accept it and get started where you are. When you accept it, you can work with it. And when you work with it, you can succeed.

You have to work with what you have. And you can learn from everything. You can grow through anything and be better off for the experience. Once you're comfortable with your reality you can live it on your own terms. And even when reality is a bad situation, by facing the truth you can respond to it properly. There's no one to blame for your life. And it's up to you to silently applaud yourself as you grow through it.

God gave you ability and you'll always have God's support. Look for it. Think about it. Ask for it. Be confident that whatever circumstances hold you back, there's wisdom inside you that knows the difference between right and wrong. Trust it and you'll turn your mind into a living expression of God's consciousness. That attitude is ready to help you. It'll enable you to make the best out of any situation. So trust God and trust yourself. You're never alone. And you're never without love.

Recognizing a Friend

A friend's love is precious. Gender doesn't matter. Kindness does. Trust, support, and acceptance make the difference. So how do you know someone's a friend? First you have to know that many people, like you, are looking for love and friendship.

Then how are you supposed to know the difference between a loving friend, a casual acquaintance, and some co-dependent person who simply craves the comfort of any human contact? A co-dependent relationship imitates support but it really trades on weaknesses where the "friends" suffer but seek security in a familiar situation. In contrast, a healthy relationship builds you up instead of usurping life's healing process. A friend won't accept your weaknesses if you're trying to maintain a position of dependency. A healthy relationship seeks you out at your greatest potential and pushes you forward towards it.

You'll know a friend by what's obvious even if you don't trust it right away. No one wants to make the mistake of giving their trust too freely only to be betrayed later. You protect yourself by using the simple cautions of your common sense. Don't blindly go into any relationship. With thoughtfulness you can enter many rewarding friendships. But at the start you'd be wise to ask yourself some questions.

SENSiBLE QUESTiONS FOR DEVELOPiNG FRiENDSHiPS

- Does this person have the same interests I do?
- Do we have similar outlooks on life?
- Do we share similar values?
- Can I trust this person to accept me when I reveal my doubts and desires?
- Are we both being honest?
- Do they appreciate me?
- Do they respect me as well as value me?
- Are they interested in my thoughts on things?
- Are they interested in my welfare?
- Am I interested in theirs?
- Do I respect them?

When you free yourself from society's opinions and accept your honest feelings then you'll create a happiness for yourself that's fun to share with your friends.

Are you ever surprised to be running into the same person every day? And it's not just at school or work, where you have to be, but everywhere. Is there a friendly face you're always bumping into around town? Or do you find people you once knew keep popping up in your life? It's because people attract those like themselves. It's not an accident. It's nature.

True friends will find a way to come together whether they know they're friends or not. So you have to trust your feelings and say, "Hello." You need to make the approach. You have to break the ice regardless of social conventions which might make you think there's something wrong with your friendship. Sometimes there are negatives involved which can be addressed and resolved if you want to. Common "stamping grounds" show a depth to a relationship that goes beyond mere acquaintances. There exists a compelling impulse in humanity, supported by the universe, to support love everywhere. And friendship is the eloquence of that love.

When your feelings about someone are real and not some contrivance you've created to boost your ego, you'll be happily surprised to find your feelings reciprocated. Like attract like. Though you've never even spoken, when you feel that you like someone—male or female—the odds are good that person likes you too. Common sense tells us, "Birds of a feather flock together." It's an old saying people still use because you can trust its timeless wisdom.

Knowing this can help you find people you want to include in your life. And you'll be able to identify those you don't want in your life too. You can understand people through their associations—what they like to do, who they like to be with, who they admire, and what they value. It's the start to seeing a person's personality.

It's a practical approach but it illuminates just a part of a person's character. A person's character reveals itself through its consistency when confronted with different situations. Like it or not, the truth is constant and reflects its identity. So if you're not sure about someone's character just be willing to face the truth and protect yourself.

Give new relationships plenty of room. You might not have a friend when you realize the person is a negative influence holding you back from your happiness. But if it isn't good for you then change it. End it. Be quick and complete. Make whatever explanations you have to, but remove yourself from a bad relationship. Then you can take a breath and feel your opportunities return.

After making a change like that you can feel lonely. Trust God that loneliness is temporary. Sometimes first you have to make room for a new relationship. You have to clear out old thoughts to give someone new an opportunity to enter your life. Then you'll be open to accept their fresh energy. Once you make that commitment you've shown your desire to grow. And you're already halfway home.

ROMANCE

Being "in love" is different. It has its own feelings. And it has its own rules. It's full of dramatic extremes, exquisite emotional highs and tragic emotional lows. What is it then? It's mysterious but it seems important. It's intense yet complicated. So you may be asking yourself, "What's this love thing everyone's always talking about?" From everything around you, you know that somehow it's the real beginning to your social maturity.

While you're trying to understand it, you're constantly meeting its reflection in popular culture. It's in music and books. It's on TV and the radio. It's at home and in the street. Being in love is *everywhere*. But if you haven't experienced it yet, it's hard to define.

You start off by seeing people deliriously happy being in love or desperately miserable having lost love. All you know is that somehow those people had bonded and were invisibly joined—even if only for a little while. When things are going right they spend all their time together. They talk to each other every day. About what, you don't know. But now they seem complete. They seem normal and perfectly positioned for their place in society. Everyone's doing it. It's definitely some coming of age thing. It's grown up, but what is it?

Your biological clock recognizes your sexual maturity. Its precise timing turns you on in anticipation of your sexual purpose. All the parts of your humanity wake up in excited harmony. But you may have difficulty describing the sensations you're having. This confusing stage of life is normal for everyone. So don't worry that you might not be ready for puberty. It'll find you. And many people have a problem accepting their body's changing messages.

Growing up is more than just being older. It's about choices, judgments, and adjustments. When you're just taking control of your life, things suddenly fall into chaos. And when you look for answers, it's common to find conflicting advice on what's happening to you and the best way to handle it.

It's obvious it's about mating. So you may think finding your mate is your salvation. You might think that through marriage you'll be saved from the desert of disinterested humanity and become a welcome member of society. You might see marriage as a shortcut to adulthood and the answer to life's growing pains. And besides that, the bliss of being in love feels great.

Falling out of Love

But loving is different than being in love. Loving is selfless where being in love gives an opportunity for selfishness to create a dependent desire for the sensation of love. And self-serving desires can be oblivious to a partner's feelings. When the truth's realized, the fall from salvation can be a terrible shock. And thoughts of loss, after being so close to happiness, can lead someone to anger and despair.

The emotional strain of losing something affects everyone differently. And their feelings can range from an emotional inconvenience to being a depressing catastrophe. Being in love has such emotional intensity that the pain of loss, like grief, can last for months or years. Sadly enough, the hurt can be so unbearable that people even explore drastic measures to relieve their pain.

Unfortunately, for some this pain is excruciating—energized by thoughts of betrayal, unworthiness, and hopelessness. It's from this terrible consciousness that thoughts can come to hurt oneself or someone else—whoever's blamed for the pain. And it's in this emotional instability that vengeance and self-hatred can drive out common sense.

It's tragic that within the power of love exists such destructiveness. Patience, kindness, and reason cure emotional pain. In the kindness of friends and family is time for nature to heal any emotional wound. So be kind *to yourself.* Be kind *to everyone.* Life goes on if you give it a chance. It's in your power to decide your future. And God will support your loving efforts.

Spirits come together in love. The love that joins two people together is bright and beautiful. That beauty comes from the core of God's consciousness. But free will allows for separation as well as coming together. And relationships end for many reasons. But other than feeling that it's right for you, no justification's needed.

A relationship needs the support of two people to be successful. And it only takes one party desiring to end the relationship for it to be over for both. The intensity of spiritual bonding perceived from a human perspective can be confusing. So being forced to leave a loving relationship can be terrifyingly frustrating. When a young relationship ends there's usually no material loss other than the loss of emotional support. But that support is essential to our neediness as we enter into maturity. Lacking experience, support's a necessity.

Your experience is your self-support. It's learning by living and respecting the value of each lesson learned. Love teaches us about life. Any time we touch it we grow. And growth shows you that you're never without love, even when it seems that way.

IT'S EASY WHEN YOU KNOW HOW.

Someone's love for you is tremendously supportive. It exposes an element of life that's always part of you. It joins your spirit to the temporal world. It's a commitment of souls working with each other to solve life's mystery. And it's the reflection of God's presence touching you.

In every relationship is a potential beyond any other experience on Earth. A loving relationship is people devoted to each other who build their lives with respect for each other as individuals. They stand up for themselves and their partner, accept themselves and their partner, and share their goals together. And they take care of each other.

APPEARANCE MATTERS

How do you know when you're in love? How are you supposed to meet your "soul mate?" Amazingly, physical appearance is an accurate indicator of compatibility. There's the old joke about people being together so long that they've started to look like each other.

Certainly the same lifestyle can do that. Whether you like living in the city, want a rural life, or prefer suburbia, the environment can produce similar effects on the people living there. It contributes to people's attitudes too. Then their thoughts and feelings become mirrored in the way they carry themselves. So their outer world, physical selves, and personalities reflect the lives they share.

There's another saying that "Opposites attract." While people do seek complementary abilities in their partners, actually the reverse is true. *Likes attract.* "Birds of a feather do flock together." So if two people's thoughts and feelings can mimic each other, why shouldn't their physical appearances be similar too? And it is that way.

You might like the looks of the tall blonde or the personality of the dark ethnic one, but you'll really resonate with people who more closely resemble yourself. People recognize each other by seeking out their mirror image, their reflection. And it goes beyond race and regional traits. It's more specific in how it matches someone's actual physical features. Living things have ways of recognizing each other. And someone like you, especially a spouse, could be very physically similar to yourself. There's a lot to see in a person's face. And your type should match you fairly well.

So, test it. Turn to the wedding announcements page in your local newspaper. Examine the faces of the partners. You'll be amazed to see the similarities and you'll see the ones who don't go together too. Often in second marriages the new partner looks like the original spouse. But it's not a re-creation of the old marriage. It just used the same tools to recognize a new opportunity. Remember, appearance doesn't guarantee success in a marriage. It indicates compatibility.

So instead of looking for some magazine dream date, open yourself to the idea of being attracted to someone who looks like you.

You could be pleasantly surprised to find that unexpected attraction enthusiastically shared by your companion. It'll be a delight for both of you. You'll be thrilled to find how much you have in common and how well you get along. So don't look for beauty. Look for harmony and you'll find beauty beyond your dreams.

SPIRITING AROUND EXERCISE

Even if you're not sure what you're looking for, here's a technique to help you. Visualizing a relationship is the same as visualizing anything you want. You're trying to focus your mind's eye and bring your feelings into solid form. It's like a game with you directing your daydreams. You picture who you are, who you're with, and what you're doing. Then you fill in the details. And you keep changing it till it's perfect. Then your dream can step out of the background and you'll know it when you see it. Just be realistic. And absolutely be generous. Remember, a relationship's a two-way street.

GETTING MARRIED

Marriage and having your own family is an important goal for many people, an interest for others, and a big question mark for the rest of us. It dominates every social perspective as a framework for society. The majority of us grow up in a family environment. Whether it's a traditional family with a mother and father, a single parent family, or a foster family, adults teach children how to live. Most communities recognize that its young members need time to grow, be educated, and have useful experiences. And a family provides the intimate supportive environment that's needed at this time. It's how we're "raised" from youth to maturity.

When marriage bonds you to a person it joins your families as well. All these new relations, once strangers, now become a part of your life. And you have to learn to manage these new relationships in a respectful balance that respects you, your family, and your extended family too.

Together with your spouse you'll find the strength you need. And with a little luck you'll find some new friends. You may find financial resources and business opportunities open for you. New people bring fresh perspectives and you'll undoubtedly find new experiences. Most precious of all, you'll get a share of the joy that comes when two people love each other.

So what's it going to cost you? You pay for it with your love, your time, your energy, and your commitment. It's more than wearing a gold ring to symbolize being grown up. It really is being grown up. And it's more than a confirmation of your love and passion. It's the acceptance of personal responsibility that comes with maturity because it's the responsibility you accept for someone else. It doesn't measure your value as a person or make you real. You're already all that. Seeking validation through marriage is just the opposite. It's a sign of immaturity and confusion.

Maturity can't be rushed. Learning nurtures maturity by providing guidance from teachers. Explanations help you make sense of your experiences. But marriage isn't an exercise. It's a legal commitment. And these legalities give it real meaning. It means you're agreeing to a partnership under the law. It means you're accepting certain responsibilities which your partner reasonably expects you to perform. And your spouse will do things because they expect certain things from you in return. With your commitment to marriage you accept personal responsibility for your actions with the knowledge that what you do directly affects your partner. Even if you're just living together, without a formal marriage contract, your actions are saying that if something's needed for the partnership you'll do it and you'll pay for it. You're promising to stand up for your marriage and work willingly to solve its problems.

Marriage is an agreement. And it's the same as any partnership agreement. But unlike a business contract where an effort's made to be specific on what the partners can expect, in a marriage contract the responsibilities are often vaguely stated and left to tradition and trust. Unfortunately this can lead to different interpretations. And for two trusting people there can still be conflicts in understanding each one's responsibilities. And it often depends on a person's priorities when they're young and still developing their values.

DEALiNG WiTH DiVORCE

When a marriage ends without an agreement the antagonists will naturally interpret the law in the spirit of their own survival—not in the spirit of fairness. The result can be a "messy divorce." Even if things weren't thought out before, both parties are still legally bound by their original agreement.

So you may need a lawyer to get out of a marriage. And the divorce process can be painfully expensive, both financially and emotionally. And it can eat away your time while you're forced to address problems you can't ignore. Where children are concerned, your relationship to your ex never ends. It'll follow you around the rest of your life in the responsibility you share to your kids. So memories of your past relationship will always be a part of your present-day life.

It can be a burden you wish wasn't there. But you'll have to live with it and make the best of it whether you like it or not.

When pressures on a marriage create conflicts greater than the marriage can endure then divorce may be the best solution. Sometimes it's best to live as separate individuals and seek happiness independently. Then, enabled by your freedom, you can be your own person again without suffering the continued limitations of an exhausting relationship.

Separate your lives and start over again. Separate your goals and dream your dreams again. Separate your money and begin again.

CHILDREN & DIVORCE

The responsibilities of parenthood never end. And the way a divorce affects children can present problems which you probably wish would just go away. They don't though. And, unfortunately for you, you'll have to deal with them from your children's point of view.

Your children will need your guidance to help them through life. Like you they must face life's challenges. A child's journey is bound to include health problems, value challenges, and tests of their emotional strength. And basic to being a parent is your financial responsibility to your children. Having enough money to pay the bills is an issue at any age. So think what it means to be young, new to the ways of the world, and without anyone to rely on. Meeting grown-up responsibilities alone can make life unmanageable. That's what parents are for.

Even after a divorce, your duty to your kids is unavoidable. Your children will always be an important part of your life. And that responsibility is with you every day for the rest of your life. Life's problems may seem unfair. But good parenting makes them bearable. So your children will always need your love and support regardless of your marital status.

Separate your minds and bodies and breathe again. Don't deny yourself. Don't suffer. Be brave and love yourself again.

Whether or not you agree with a court's decision, there's finality in the dissolution of a marriage. But thoughts and feelings can take a long time to heal. The human mind exists in a complex paradigm of interactivity and responsibility. And failure forces us to painful self-examination. Just keep in mind that the purpose in self-examination is improvement, not judgment.

Too young

Societies' laws set limits on the age a person has to be to get married. If a person's considered a minor, below the age of lawful consent, then they need permission from a parent or guardian to marry. And if you think it's an arbitrarily chosen age, you're right. But it's not an arbitrary decision. Age requirements are intended to protect inexperienced young people from making bad decisions that they'll have to live with the rest of their lives. Age limits are established by politicians, adult leaders whose responsibility it is to set policies that serve everyone in the community.

Adults have experience with life. They're familiar with basic human nature and they've seen the mistakes inexperience can make. Their job is to determine a fair and responsible age when a young person can be expected to have matured enough to make sensible decisions. This gives young people a chance to grow up because it recognizes their limited exposure to life's responsibilities.

It's the same as having a minimum age for driving a car, drinking liquor, or being liable to business contracts. The community understands that young people may not be fully aware of the results of their actions. And the community wants to support all its citizens.

It knows that what affects an individual can affect the whole community. An immature driver may be exhilarated by the excitement of driving fast without realizing the pain and suffering that a traffic accident can cause. Or the pleasures of materialism may be too much to resist for someone young while their indulgence can create a deep financial hole for someone just starting out in life. And consensual sex by minors can bring unwanted pregnancies and the unplanned for responsibilities of parenthood which could have been avoided had they given themselves time to understand it better.

When a young person acts irresponsibly their problems fall on society to fix. Age limits help the community help its young citizens move through this difficult phase where their experience hasn't caught up to their abilities yet.

Maturity is a sense of personal responsibility that develops from your experiences seen over time. It's important to understand the world and see how your actions affect it. We all mature at different ages and a reasonable society knows it. Societies mature too. And as they do they try to set age limits that respect a young person's right to enjoy life in a flexible enough environment where the community's life is respected too. This is the moral consideration that gives young people the best chance for success by helping them avoid predictable problems. The community's role in parenting helps young people enter society as a positive influence with their full potential intact.

Laws that set limits aren't meant to restrict free expression. They're intended to create fairness for the whole community so everyone has the same freedom to live in harmony with their neighbors. Laws that set age limits are like roadside warning signs. The signs might read "Slippery When Wet", "Slow Curve", or "School Zone 15 MPH." It's because the responsibility of the people who build the roads is to make sure those roads are safe to travel. Their authority is needed to protect the public and keep everyone informed about possible dangers to their driving. If it wasn't necessary then flashing lights with ringing bells would be enough warning at railroad crossings for motorists to stop. But human nature shows us that it's not enough. That's why we need crossing gates, physical barriers lowered to block the way of any motorist who ignores the warnings and tries to beat the train across the tracks.

Age limits don't impose authority without reason. It's not power for ego's sake. It's a community's responsibility to provide their young people with guidance. No one likes strangers telling them what to do. But no matter how frustrated you may feel, remember that a healthy community tries to be fair. Regardless of age, regulations in a benevolent society are designed for everyone's benefit. And rules are made for those who want to get along with their neighbors to be able to do it without interference.

So decisions must be made on where to draw the line that balances a conflict. The problem is in making a fair compromise. And the question is always, "Who's going to give up what?" Then we have to live with it in a practical way. Age limits are adjusted to accommodate social growth. Voting ages have been lowered out of respect for youth's growing civic awareness. The drinking age has been raised in some places as more was learned about the tragic costs of traffic accidents caused by inexperienced young people whose judgment and driving skills had been impaired by alcohol. And marriage is just as important. Beyond a couple's personal relationship, marriage is a statement to society.

4 SECRETS FOR A SUCCESSFUL MARRIAGE

Secret #1: Don't expect your spouse to be your savior. If being coddled or rescued is your reason for getting married then you'll burden your partner and disappoint yourself. This mistake can lead to conflicts between you and your spouse. One-sided expectations don't make sense where mutual support's the basis for a relationship. Don't assume that it's part of your partner's responsibilities to be your healer. This trap is real. But it's easily hidden under the carpet of everyday life. Honest communication is how you find acceptance in a marriage. And that's where you'll find your support.

Secret #2: The bottom line is patience. Patience takes time to think things through calmly. It's not avoiding a decision. It's being smart about it. You can go as far as you can in your relationship with what you know. But your patience should be satisfied before you make a commitment. Take time to consider the alternatives. Every choice is a different road and every value has a different balance. So take your time! You won't be missing anything. Your new family is too important to start without thinking about it. If you really want to get married then wait. You might avoid an early divorce or winding up as a stressed out single parent.

Secret #3: There are times when your partner won't be there for you. Even when things are great, marriage can be challenging. Life pressures you both and it's up to the two of you to press back with a positive attitude. When one partner's feeling bad, for whatever

COMMON SENSE COVERS MARRIAGE TOO.

Marriage and having a family is the centerpiece experience of most people's lives. And good judgment in choosing a partner and deciding when to get married are very important. So consider them carefully and take your time to make a confident choice.

4 SECRETS FOR A SUCCESSFUL MARRIAGE *(continued)*

reason, there's the love of the other to be a compassionate companion. There's the love of a spouse to be sympathetic and strong when help is needed. The challenge is when both partners are needy. There are times when a husband and wife are both worn out and unable to share what they think they don't have. They'll cry out for help but there won't be anyone there. And instead of compromising, their partner will be asking more of them when they're feeling empty themselves. It's not unusual. So don't be concerned. Problems come up when we think we're least able to deal with them. That's how life tests us. But it's manageable because God supports your love.

Secret #4: In conflicts, separate yourself from the problem and support your marriage. You're in a partnership. So listen to your partner. It's important to acknowledge a problem and not blame anyone for it. Sometimes it's hard to temper your frustration but patience is the process that solves problems. Everything about a marriage is emotional. It's as close to home as you can get. So first catch your breath when you have a problem. Then mend your own wounds. The power to heal your feelings is inside you. And once you feel better you'll be able to make the compromises that help your partner feel good too. It only takes one revitalized partner to bring balance back to a marriage. So hang on! Focus on wanting your relationship to be whole for both of you. Take time for both of you to relax. Then you'll see peace return and your love grow with it.

It's important to understand what it means to share your life with your spouse. It means sharing your goals. It means being responsible for someone other than yourself. And it could mean being a parent and raising your children together.

Again, marriage doesn't confirm you as a person. Neither is it proof of your desirability. Your value as a person is unquestionable.

But it can be a trap of frustrating entanglements so you should be clear on everyone's expectations before you get married. Your decision won't affect only you. It'll directly affect your partner, your families, and your children as well.

A loving spouse can give you joy and comfort. And sharing being in love is fun. Being a parent can give you love and happiness beyond your dreams. You just have to be ready for it and want it more than anything else.

ARE YOU READY TO BE A PARENT?

Your responsibility to your children is absorbing and unending. A child's needs must be met. They depend on you. Children can't wait till their needs fit your schedule. So life won't be at your convenience anymore. What your child needs will be the dominant part of your daily schedule, including your plans for the future.

As your children grow up it'll be your responsibility to protect them, give them a home, and direct them. It'll be up to you to show them how to take care of themselves—be safe, productive, and get along with others. Are you ready for that? Do you want to do it? *Be sure.* You're taking on the biggest responsibility of your life.

Parenthood is where joy and responsibility meet. And once you go down that road you can't go back. You'll find pressures on your time and energy that can stretch you to your breaking point. And when you do break you'll have to find ways to fix yourself and go on—for you and your family. If you still want it and you're ready for the commitment, even with the sacrifices you make, the rewards can be awesome. And many people find it well worth the effort.

But be careful when you have children. You should feel a measure of satisfaction with what you've already accomplished in life. You should feel basically complete. You should feel that you've done most of the things you wanted to try. You shouldn't feel that you're limiting yourself by being a parent. Whatever you do from then on you'll do as a family. And once you have a family it could be a while before you have an opportunity to follow another one of your dreams.

THE IMPORTANCE OF LOVING YOURSELF

Love is self-love too. You should love yourself for who you are. You should love what you do. You can love politics, sports, or religion. You can love working or watching TV. You can love shopping, studying, or being with friends. It's because with anything in life it's enjoying the experience that matters.

How you feel about what you're doing is what's important. It's the pleasure you have in your thoughts when you think about the things you like. Because whatever you do, you love how you relate to it. And when you touch the part of you that gives you joy, you love yourself. You discover who you are as you're reflected in life's details. Then you can recognize yourself. You're an expressive human being. And when you stop worrying about what others may think, you release yourself from any limits other than your soul's self-respect. And you can have a great time doing what you like.

Your happiness exists in life. But sometimes you have to be brave to release your happiness and expose who you are to the world. We all see life in our own way. And we should all take advantage of it.

You have to trust what fascinates you and touches your soul. It could be your participation in a heated debate or the comfort you find in reading. Whatever it is, it's a sign of who you are. And when you love who you are, you complete yourself. You become a center of symmetry in the universe. And you achieve the balance and focused power that go with it.

So be genuine. Trust your nature. It's there to help you. And the harmony you find in accepting yourself should be the inspiration you need for overcoming any doubts.

LOVE FOR YOUR COMMUNITY

Love for your country and community makes you part of a greater whole. It's the unified greatness of civilization. Civilization is a state of mind where you live together in peace with your neighbors. There we find safety and self-respect in our common goals. And there you can love who you are as being part of something bigger than just yourself.

There's security in citizenship. It means you're not alone. You're sympathetic. You know how people feel because you feel the same thing. So it's easier to be comfortable with people who've had the same experiences as you. Together you share a history of challenges and achievements. And when these experiences are joined they form the nexus of the culture you share.

In important ways the people you live with mirror who you are. You can easily recognize the common traits you share. The union of your lives is a product of your common history. That makes it easy for you to sympathize with your neighbors' dreams and tribulations. It's only when you respect your neighbors that you really love yourself because self-love is the same for everyone. So when you respect your neighbors you respect yourself.

With all your experience in questioning who you are you find an example of your relationship to God. Belonging to larger and larger groups mimics our relationship to God as it brings us closer to the one variety we call the universe. That's why we proudly love our country, our community, or any group we passionately give our heart. You love yourself as part of the group that stands for what you believe in.

LOVE FOR GOD

Love for God is the conscious effort to find reason and meaning in life. It's the same whether you seek God's wholeness through kindness and good works, devotion through self-sacrifice, or the search for truth in God's nature. And what's been described as a thirst for truth is as much a part of your life as water. The proof is in the presence of the world's religions.

The variety of religious concepts reflects the different opportunities God's given us to understand ourselves as a part of nature. Through different religions God is seen in ways that allow every culture to understand God's nature and apply it specifically to their own experience. There are many religions and within them separate sects with their own beliefs. Together they give dimensions to God's definition. And this wealth of ideas allows choices for souls to explore themselves.

Regardless of practice, religions are a testament to God's perspective. So God's appearance varies in religions' explorations. How we see religion and its limitations are revealed in the simple story of the blind men who tried to describe an elephant just by using their sense of touch.

The first blind man touched the elephant's long trunk and described it as being like a snake. The second one felt the elephant's thick legs and described it as being like a tree. The third one held the elephant's big ears and described it as having wings. As each blind man

GOD EVOLVES

Religions evolve through civilization's maturity. By studying our beliefs we learn what we can about God. And we evolve as that knowledge affects us. Spiritual effort has focus so religion is never just a mindless thing we do. Religions are uncovered paths of discovery. And discovering that you have a soul is an accomplishment. But discovery is never complete because it expands into new creations. Know that we all come together in love. Where we go individually is a personal matter.

touched a different part of the creature they came away with a different understanding. With separate perspectives and that single sense of awareness they did their best to describe it. But their evaluations were incomplete. And they misunderstood the animal's nature. Likewise a limited life experience can lead to an incomplete picture of God. This demonstrates the difficulty in describing something just by examining a part of it. It's important to see the whole picture. To know the whole richness of God, start with love and acknowledge it everywhere.

There's more to understanding life than just one viewpoint. So open your mind to accept new perceptions. Remember the story of the blind men and the elephant. When they got together they saw how their separate experiences fit the whole picture. And the elephant showed its true form. Combined, their experiences had an accurate sense of the creature's identity. By assembling the separate parts they were able to piece together a picture of what an elephant really is. And as they understood how the parts worked together, they understood more about the elephant's needs and potential.

One way or another we're all trying to understand God. And we take the road our cultures lead us. Like the blind men, we look at life through a small hole in the fence of awareness—our personalities. Simply by living we're compelled to it. You can't avoid it. It's your conscience. It's the part of God you are. It demands that you acknowledge your life with love as your birthright. Love for God is your love for your soul and the life you make for it. It's your guide to right and wrong.

Loving God is the essence of faith and believes that God is real and has a purpose for you. Loving God is freedom from the thousands of thoughts that overwhelm us in self-importance. Loving God is accepting yourself as part of the goodness and everlasting love that makes you who you are. And it knows you're unfailingly supported in everything you do.

Loving God is the desire to know, directly from the source, what your values should be. Loving God is the desire to know the value of material things. Loving God seeks the meaning of materiality as well as it seeks the meaning of loving your neighbor. God sees your relationships and questions you on them. They include everything from your feelings about your family to how you feel about people on the other side of the world. Loving God is the desire to know your relationship to your planet, its life, and its nature. Loving God is the desire to know justice as it seeks balance in every relationship. And it seeks to know the boundaries that bless every experience. Loving God is a desire to know the meaning of service. And know the difference between selfishness, selflessness, and self-respect. In all, loving God seeks self-knowledge so we can honor our responsibilities.

Loving God sees you as God alive. Loving God is the complex simplicity in seeing yourself apart from others while at the same time you're complete with everyone you meet. And loving God wants right thoughts and actions to be your priorities in overcoming life's resistance.

We all love God in a personal way. And we worship God in accord with God's plan for us. We all do it perfectly well too. And we all have the same problem of trying to figure out why life confounds us so much. To love God is to let your best intentions be your guide. Your intentions are your spiritual self. And your spiritual self is your connection between you, God, and the world. It's a sense of who you are that's more than your humanity. And it expands when you limit life's attempts to contain it.

Reasonably so, we're confused by life's conflicts. We know every human being is an aspect of God. And through love we know that God keeps an infinite equilibrium in creation. So in every conflict there's an opportunity to serve God and restore that equilibrium. It means that you can't avoid doing what's right. Everything points you in that direction.

Think About It — Chapter 4

Thought #1: *Love and sex are mysteries full of pain and joy. There are as many explanations for love as there are people to have them.*

Thought #2: *To avoid the pitfalls that can affect your sexual experience, your best protection will always be good advice and the patience to learn what you can about your own sexuality—one of the most complex responsibilities in life.*

Thought #3: *Love is the fabric of experience. Simply put, it's important and it matters. And it matters more than anything else.*

Thought #4: *Marriage, for many, is the most important experience in their lives. So it makes sense to consider your decision carefully and take as much time as you need to feel confident in your choice.*

Thought #5: *A loving God sees you as God alive. So, loving God accepts responsibility in meeting your everyday problems.*

WHEN A CONTROVERSY COMES UP,
THE FIRST THING WE WANT TO KNOW
IS "WHAT'S THE TRUTH?"
AND THEN, "WHAT'S THE RIGHT
THING TO DO ABOUT IT?"

TO UNDERSTAND WHAT'S RIGHT, IT'S
IMPORTANT TO REALIZE THAT
THERE CAN BE MORE THAN ONE RIGHT
ANSWER TO A QUESTION.

CHAPTER 5

CoNFLicts & CoNtroversies

This is about right and wrong because we often run into different opinions about it. And sometimes you can find yourself on both sides of an issue. Or you might have a firm opinion on one side while someone else is just as convinced the truth is the opposite. Or something you feel is very important might be considered inconsequential by someone else, or vice versa. Sometimes you'll have the majority's point of view and other times you'll share the minority's disappointment. These are life's controversies because individuality means everyone has their own opinion. And their values can be different.

A wide range of issues affect you personally or as a member of a community wrestling to decide what its values should be. It's important because it's about what a society permits, which activities are limited, and what's not allowed at all.

In a free society we try to draw reasonable borders that respect everyone. These are the limits that give individuals their freedom of expression while allowing society to enjoy its own expression too. It's about mutual respect and compromising to find a way to live together without interfering with each other. Add into the mix the differences of national heritage, economic environment, and religious doctrine then divide by 5 billion people and it's a wonder that we get along as well as we do.

Living by the Rules

The first rule of life is "Live and let live." But when boundaries are crossed, or thought to be crossed, conflicts can occur. When a controversy comes up, the first thing anyone wants to know is "What's the truth?" And then, "What's the right thing to do about it?" To understand what's right it's important to realize that there can be more than one right answer to a question.

Every solution has unique qualities that are agreeable to some and disagreeable to others. That means it's important to have policies that, at least, address the needs of the minority when a decision is made to serve the greater good of the community. Some people aren't going to get what they want while others are favored. However, in a community relationship it should never be all or nothing. There should always be an effort to do what can be done for everyone out of respect for the whole community.

Rules should be flexible enough to serve society's changing needs. Rules are for guidance. Laws are the social agreements we make so the guidance can be enforced for everyone's benefit. What the law allows affects you. It can limit what you do. Or it can affect you sympathetically when you feel someone's being treated unfairly.

Feelings about the things that affect us indirectly can be deeply personal because they touch our sense of justice. Or with no cost to ourselves we have the luxury of unencumbered feelings about the outcome. When we're not directly affected it's easier to accept a point of view even when it isn't true. Anything's okay. So what?

Being apart from a situation makes it easier to reject a compromise. Where irresponsible thinking doesn't cost anything we often see no point in being reasonable. Our emotions can be more intense because we don't have to deal with the facts. We become spectators seeing the events as entertainment instead of the real life situations someone else has to live.

The truth is everything affects you. Your perspective on life continually affects you. It's personal and immediate. Life has a way of catching up with us. What once seemed remote can suddenly jump up and before you know it you're totally involved.

AN APPROACH TO CONFLICT

Conflict comes when our sense of security is threatened. This includes the safety we feel in groups, whether it's our race, politics, or anything else we associate with. Religious conflicts are especially intense because the differences are about our responsibilities to life and what we believe is the right way to respect God. The odd thing about religious differences is that they're more about style than anything else. At some point all religions come together in God's love.

All sides will have justifications to explain a conflict. How defensible you find their opinions depends on your point of view and sense of fairness. But tolerance asks that we expand our perspectives to include everyone. With the right formula we can all contribute to society. Excluding anyone limits us. And we confine ourselves to a fortress mentality when we keep others at a distance. While there's security in a community, your love for your neighbors shouldn't limit your opportunity. With all its confusing variety, humanity's still your true identity even if it takes courage to accept it.

Love's the difference between right and wrong. It unites us in common sense, the common ground for everyone's thinking. But decisions move to the will of power and "might makes right." But what makes might? It's not military or political power. Real power is God's righteousness. Policies can change but God's purpose is constant.

God's expression on Earth is civilization. Civilization matures as a single unit made of many parts that depend on each other. And it recreates itself with the spirit of its new generations. So there's always something solid to hold on to, something new to learn, and something empty to fill with fresh dreams.

Take a Stand.

Abortion is a controversy with heated points of view on all sides. Is abortion baby killing or a sensible way to end an unwanted pregnancy? Is it murder or reproductive freedom? Would a soul even have an interest in an aborted fetus or is the potential for any human experience sacred? When more than one life is at risk, whose is more important? Do modern methods of abortion and birth control make it too easy to avoid the moral concerns? Is it an intellectual argument or is the issue something that should be legislated for everyone's benefit? The point is you shouldn't take sides on an issue till you take time to consider it fairly based on your own opinion.

To start you have to free yourself from the threatening rhetoric. You have to find a safe place in your mind where you can rise above the "We're right! You're wrong!" protestations and learn from your own inner wisdom what feels right for you. Your calm mind will see through the insistent advertising, expert opinions, and selected testimonials. When you set your mind to it you'll see past the lies and mistakes. And you'll ask the right questions.

Whatever an advertisement promotes you can be sure it'll be done with authority and conviction. You'll find images that tug at your heart and statistics to impress you. They all have the same purpose though—to manipulate your beliefs to agree with them. So, keep a degree of skepticism about what other people promote. And trust yourself. Depend on the wisdom God gave you. Look at the simple facts on both sides. Then decide what you'll believe.

Now what? You may find yourself with a new challenge. What if your feelings on the right thing to do conflict with your neighbors? What if your honest opinion is different than the community consensus? Should you keep quiet or challenge the majority? Thinking outside the group can be uncomfortable. And it can be a real dilemma when you've considered something carefully. It's common for the group opinion to resist new ideas. So it takes courage to honor yourself, stand by your convictions, and defend your reality. But self-respect is the only road to harmony in life.

INDiViDUXL RiGHTS VS. THE GOOD OF SOCiETy

A constant controversy is the conflict between an individual's right to self-expression and the government's power to restrict those rights. Like two sides of a spinning coin these issues combine to keep balance in a fluid relationship. The government supports its citizens safely within its framework so they can live as individuals who benefit society.

So it's important to be fair. Real personal success respects society. It walks the line between self-interest and fairness. This contradiction challenges us to create rules that are fair to everyone in cost and benefit. This is what it means to be a human being. And it's the same way everywhere.

And it can get complicated. For instance, should someone who's been adopted have the right to know their birth parents if the original decision was that their child should never know? It's hard to understand the strange solitude of an adopted person's yearning to know their origins. If life's treated them well, if they're healthy, and have a good family, it's hard to see why they should feel something's missing. Yet they do have those feelings. And those feelings should be respected. They want to know their roots. They want to know their history. It's a part of their psyche they can't complete. But where are the protections for unwed teen mothers or families without the means to take care of a baby? Will they be allowed the security of their secret? Can they move on with their lives after suffering the terrible doubts that justify why they've given their baby away to a stranger? Will we let them have a life without reliving the guilt of leaving their child behind? The real question is how we respect the affected parties. Hopefully time is kind to everyone. In these situations, God willing, we hope we mature to see everyone's needs met and find love where we are.

A COMPLEX CONFLICT

Being pulled in opposite directions by ideas competing with each other is confusing at best. Everyone wants to do the right thing. Everyone wants to take care of themselves, respect their neighbors, and contribute to society. But it's important to remember that people can have ulterior motives and subconscious agendas for an issue. And the way a matter resolves affects us feeling right about it.

It doesn't matter whether you're for or against something. There will always be someone, from either side, ready to raise the emotional ante. They'll do it out of belief, manipulation, or a combination of the two. Remember, belief isn't founded in the truth so much as it's founded in sincerity. And passionate words and dramatic pictures aren't always the truth as much as they're meant to be the proof that unifies the fears and frustrations of a community.

Confusion, mistaken analysis, and inaccurate details (honest mistakes or lies) all get added to the mix. These complications make it harder to understand the cause and effect of a situation—or the best way to deal with it. They can mask reality and mislead you. So you have to learn to trust yourself and seek the clarity that connects you to God. God's explanations shine through the questions that obscure everything in life. But you have to look for them.

Relying on emotions alone is a wild ride. They become vain entertainment instead of a desire for the truth. They feed on self-aggrandizement and greed. And they promote a chaotic blur that distorts opportunities for compromise. When you trust yourself you'll find co-operation is the way everyone gets what they want.

By the nature of agreements some solutions won't satisfy everyone. Even so, compromise carries the promise of love's guidance to settle arguments and create peace. Your job is to sift through the rhetoric and avoid stumbling on becoming a cynic. And your payoff will be a practical perspective that can guide you through life successfully.

It's our nature to see things differently. When you see that as an advantage your opportunities will grow. And you'll be wiser. So look for the basics. Stay with the facts. Look at the source of your information. Trust your feelings. Trust God. And ask yourself these questions the next time you're faced with a controversy:

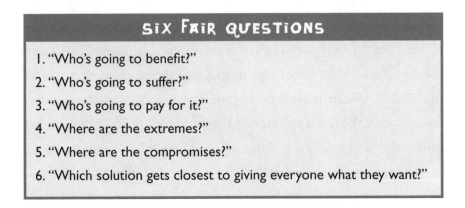

SIX FAIR QUESTIONS

1. "Who's going to benefit?"
2. "Who's going to suffer?"
3. "Who's going to pay for it?"
4. "Where are the extremes?"
5. "Where are the compromises?"
6. "Which solution gets closest to giving everyone what they want?"

The next issues are timeless and important to the way we think about ourselves. So here are some thoughts to help you form your opinions.

WAR

As a nation we prize our traditions. Though different than our neighbors our culture gives us a comfortable place to live our lives. And when we feel our comfort threatened we'll do anything to protect it. Or when our cultural identity is challenged we'll fight to preserve it. It's not a judgment over whose culture is better. While there can be extremes in cultural manners there must be respectful limitations between them so they can live together peacefully. It's the consideration for each other's cultural freedom. And cultural freedom is so important to people that they would kill or die to defend it.

Then when should a country go to war? When's a situation so threatening that we should call on our friends and neighbors to kill and die for us? When does it make sense to kill people, risk death and injury, destroy what others have built, and accept human suffering? There are valid reasons to go to war and defend ourselves but on what values should we decide?

The conflicts that bring on a war involve a real or perceived threat to our security. Our nation must be protected. But if murder—the unlawful and deliberate taking of another person's life—is so repulsive to human consciousness, we can't avoid personal responsibility when we institutionalize murdering people who live in another country. So to be responsible human beings when confronted by such grievous matters it's essential to know the true nature of the threat before we condone that murder be done in our names.

NO COMFORT, NO QUARTER

War is about deprivation. People fear they're going to lose something they need to survive. The fighting can be over resources, identity, or to remove some obstacle a country feels blocks its purpose. Ironically some wars have no higher purpose than a robbery or more meaning than playing a game.

Whatever the reason, a country acts with violence in a desire for its destiny. People choose war as the absolute way to force their will on others. The method is to kill people to eliminate opposition, destroy their production so they can't fight back, and destroy their way of life to intimidate them out of resisting. Beyond the rhetoric, war is just shortsighted selfishness with callous indifference to anything but victory. All wars start with an act of violence and escalate until one of the parties finds it intolerable and gives up. Some come to it easily. Others, responding to terrible events, must force themselves to it.

A DiViDED SOUL

Making war on ourselves confounds the human spirit. And more people believe in peace than trust the success that comes from warring on their neighbors. The thing about war is you're only as successful as your last victory. And it just takes one loss to lose everything.

Human beings want to love each other. When nations decide on war they should ask themselves, "Is war the only answer?" The truth of war's tragedy lacks appreciation for the potential we have in cooperation. It's important to keep our fear of its horrors fresh in our minds. And remember the irretrievable losses we condemn ourselves to when we choose armed conflict as our way to resolve differences.

The Warrior's Burden

We love our warriors. Their courage protects us. So it's ironic how the people we oblige to do the killing—our young warriors —have the least responsibility for the murders. It's the job we give them—pulling the triggers and pushing the buttons. Warriors don't have a choice. Military discipline demands they follow orders. That makes it the most difficult job there is. The warrior's choice is to follow orders or go to prison. But as citizens in a democracy we do have a choice. We can say yes or no to the tragedy of war. And no matter which course the majority chooses, you still have a right to your opinion.

But it's the warrior—with no freedom of choice on the battlefield—who experiences the most stress and sense of personal responsibility for the horrors of war. Besides constantly confronting their instinct for survival, they live daily with the immediacy of death, destruction, and despair. They live in an environment where innocent people suffer catastrophic losses through others' mistakes. Honest mistakes happen in any endeavor, including war. But the stress is magnified when life and death hang in the balance of simple decisions.

Warriors must kill or be killed. And every day they join their comrades in the same conflict. They may feel out of control, forced to stay in an awful place without permission to leave. Their comfort is their love for their families and their comrades. It's their duty to their country and their honor to themselves. But beyond that they may feel there's no refuge to help them reclaim the comfort of their humanity. In war young minds have always struggled searching for the reason of their place in it all.

Not a "Made for TV" Movie

It's different for those who send the troops off to wreak destruction on strangers. It's ironic how those responsible for the violence—the governments and public—can ignore its sad reality. What's worse, they get distracted and unfeeling to the human suffering. We enjoy the spectacle of war as if it was some exciting video game or "made for TV" movie instead of the terrible horror it is. It's so unspeakable we don't even want to know the truth.

Think for a minute on the reality of war. It's more than 10 minutes of TV on the evening news. Somewhere it's twenty-four hours a day every day. What if it was your street where the tanks were firing? What if it was your parents, your kids, or your friends being blown apart and burned? Think about those you love and the life you enjoy. Then look at war's realities. Think about the violence and devastation that are a part of people's lives somewhere. Think about them when you wake up tomorrow, where they are, and where you are. And don't forget it.

Sharing the Cost

War is a terrible thing. But if it's right to go to war then the burden should be shared by everyone. We should all feel the hardship and know we stand together in the fight to defeat our enemies. How can we leave our troops alone to suffer war's privations? If a war is worth fighting then the whole country should be mobilized in a practical effort. This would bring the burden of war directly into our daily lives where we could act responsibly about it. But it's easier to disconnect from the truth. We're thrilled by the power but we don't want to feel the pain. If a war's important to our survival then it should be fought as a national sacrifice, not an adventure. Some of us will suffer dreadfully so we must all respect its necessity.

Whenever we go to war we must acknowledge what we're doing. It's an awesome responsibility to intentionally kill another human being. We should all feel the pressure of it. Spiritual relief from war only comes when we accept personal responsibility for it.

DRUGS

The media create ways for us to relax and get away from the pressures of life. Newspapers, magazines, movies, TV, the radio, and the internet all provide welcome diversions. They give us a chance to change our focus from what's needed to live to what's fun about living. It's a sensory vacation. Watching the busy images on TV, moving with the rhythm of the music on the radio, or juggling the information on the internet, we hypnotize ourselves into peaceful coexistence with the world. We relax in the temporary relief of our distractions.

Taking drugs to change your mood is like that too. Whether the drugs were designed for that purpose or the mood change is a side effect, drugs can cause reactions that modify your perception. Some drugs calm us down. Others energize us. And like a good movie they can distract us from our responsibilities. But some people think they can take drugs to escape all their responsibilities. They neglect to see how misuse deadens their mind's power with a chemical shroud.

Sometimes getting high feels like freedom, like nothing can stop you, and nothing else matters beyond that moment. And it feels good to be free of your inhibitions. A part of you you've contained, a part of you you've liked, is free again and you love it.

And it's cool. You can show off your fearlessness when you enter the "forbidden zone." You're young and you want to experience everything that's out there. But mature people warn you that some things are too dangerous. You should know that some pains in life are avoidable when you use common sense. So give credit to the volumes of information that tell you how drugs can hurt you. But problems may seem distant when you're having fun being stoned. The truth is when you use magic potions to remove life's challenges you're right in the middle of a problem.

A chemically altered consciousness blinds you to your positive inhibitions too. Some inhibitions are practical and protect you from danger. Like when your subconscious tells you, "You're driving too fast!" or "Don't get too close to the edge!"

Freed from inhibitions your unleashed power may be hard to control. And you might act out your confused thoughts. You might act inappropriately in public disrespecting those around you. You might be unnaturally rude or reveal a secret told to you in trust. You might challenge yourself with dangers beyond your abilities or avoid challenges well within your ability. When drugs and alcohol suppress your inhibitions they ignore the strength you have for creating your own happiness—your capable mind.

Hiding from Life

Drug abuse uses drugs to avoid your conscious life. You try to fool yourself and escape into a vacuum of peaceful ignorance far away from your troubles. And some people can abuse drugs to the point they lose their self-control to a drug's powerful physical and psychological influences. This loss of self-control becomes self-abuse.

Self-control means you trust yourself. It means you have confidence in what you can do. Self-esteem means you accept yourself. And that you're kind to yourself. But when you don't feel right about it you'll look for that affirmation somewhere else. The problem with being young is you're still trying to make sense of the world and decide what you want, but you don't know how to do it yet. And it takes years to acquire the life skills you'll need. So it's frustrating.

Knowledge comes with time but the pain of impatience is immediate. So people look for immediate solutions to youthful frustrations. That's why people turn to drugs and alcohol. It's fast relief from the emotional pain of life's problems. On drugs, feeling successful only needs the time it takes to get high.

Emotional pains are real. And you can't rely on experience to help you sort out your broken feelings. You don't have enough of it yet. If there's someone who understands your predicament you can go to them for help. But since good guidance isn't always there, street drugs and alcohol are commonly used to cure hurt feelings.

Obviously, drugs won't solve your daily problems. Just the opposite, taking drugs makes things worse because your problems fester while you're stoned. When you take drugs you're avoiding your responsibility to solve your problems. Drugs separate the part of your mind that recognizes your responsibilities from the part that gives you comfort. So for a little while you can shut off your thoughts and feelings.

But the drugs wear off and your responsibilities return. You think about your problems again so you try to shut them down by taking more drugs. So, life becomes a cycle of addiction and then collapses as you gradually give away all self-control to a drug habit. And without constant care, your life grows weeds like any untended garden.

A Costly Diversion

Even if getting high was just a hobby it'd be an expensive one. Drugs and alcohol cost money. And most of these drugs are against the law. That makes them expensive because they're only available illegally. And when you're getting high you're not using your time making money or investing in your future. Instead, you're spending your money trying to make it through each day without any pain. But the reality is you're adding to your suffering.

What have you ever achieved while you were stoned? Relief? Maybe. But what did it cost you? The price was a clear mind that could have helped you solve the very problem causing you pain. Worst of all, you waste your time. It's precious time you could be using to help yourself heal your feelings. Once you do that you can go beyond solving your everyday problems to solving the mystery of your life. You can solve your mystery and give yourself the love waiting for you.

IT'S EVERYONE'S PROBLEM.

We affect our surroundings because human beings depend on each other. So when we have a problem it's important to fix it so it doesn't affect our neighbors. Problems grow. And your problems can affect the people in your community as much as they affect the people who love you. And you can't avoid your responsibilities to either of them. Life constantly reminds you. People send you bills in the mail. Or they ask you to do things you don't want to do. But if you can't take care of yourself you have to live somehow. So your problems become everyone's problem because we all have a stake in each other's success. And everyone counts.

When you're drunk or high on drugs your life stays in gear but there's no one to steer it. It has no direction without your intention where to go with it. In oblivion your life can swerve into any obstacle and you won't be able to stop it. And when you start off track, life's even harder as today's fast pace and competition leave you behind.

But self-medication isn't the answer when you're looking for confidence. And you can't always outsmart things or exercise the problems away. So you have to protect your emotional health when your mind's under pressure. It's your main support. So talk to a professional if you need help. Your decision to seek a counselor's advice makes good sense when you're overwhelmed. It shows that you have the self-control to fix your own problems even when the problem is you.

Your financial situation doesn't matter. Doctor's fees are cheaper than street drugs. And there are modern medicines that can help you keep your life on track without you being too stoned to work. So it's important to find a doctor who can diagnose you and prescribe the right treatment. Then you can work through your everyday problems like everyone else. Needing psychological help is not a shameful weakness. So grow up! If you feel life's more than you can handle, get professional help.

Face to Face with Peer Pressure

In life, we all want answers. And it's our peers, who we have the most in common with, who we trust the most. With today's growth in communication we're less supervised by loving parents because they can't keep up with everything. Instead we're often thrown in with strangers and unfamiliar authority figures. This naked introduction to the freedom of modern living can develop into "peer pressure" or "being cool." It's a normal part of life that grows into "keeping up with the Joneses" or "being chic." It's how human beings build social harmony by sharing standards of behavior. And we get the confirmation we're doing well when we're accepted. But if you think taking drugs measures your acceptance, you're wrong. It's no particular honor because it doesn't really take much to do. And "being popular" for it only validates your self-worth by immature people who are trying to grow up themselves.

As a young adult you start to realize the power of your independence. You see how you affect the world around you. But you're still learning the process of becoming the self-loving, self-reliant person you want to be. Till then, popularity is something we use to prove we're worthy of society. It's the reinforcement we need when we're confronted with responsibilities. But peer pressure imposes club rules on the social allure of drinking and drugs. While it starts out exploring adulthood, taking drugs can become a badge of group membership. So it's easier to keep doing it.

A FOLLOWER

There's some safety in being a follower. You could be somebody's sidekick led around willingly because you don't know what to do for yourself. You could be in a clique where multiple leaders form a super-personality that leads the whole group. Or, you might be led by an organized movement with a religious or political theme as its central belief. These are all within the escapist's plan for safety in ignorance. In ignorance you make a responsible choice to be dependent and irresponsible. That someone else will make your decisions for you. It doesn't matter if they're right or wrong. Your only thought is to avoid responsibility for making your own decisions—because you don't know how.

But when somebody else makes your decisions they decide the value of your life. When you're dependent on an artificial image of responsibility your self-worth becomes whatever the other person says it should be. But in truth you never lose your self-esteem. It's your natural condition to be whole and self-loving. So it must be a deliberate choice to give away your personal authority. And you have to force your attention away from yourself to surrender that responsibility. But because it's a choice you can always make a different choice.

When you resign your self-worth to someone else's opinion you might find relief in diverting your thoughts. But in your heart you'll always know it's an illusion of what you want. Developing self-esteem is part of growing up. But a drug culture lifestyle of "Forget tomorrow, just have fun." stifles that growth. It embraces irresponsibility and limits your opportunities.

Drugs set you adrift on life's strange currents but without a captain or destination. And they suppress the inner fire of God's consciousness that we're trying to make a part of our lives. When you're on drugs, life's untended problems haphazardly work themselves out and there's no telling where they'll take you. It's usually far from where you started, and much farther from your goals than if you had sought out sober guidance at your moments of decision. Whatever happens, you're still responsible for your life.

Carefree?

Inhibitions are life's uncertainties supported by your decision to avoid the things you doubt. People try to lose their inhibitions by getting high because it feels good to release the control their fears had over them. But they're often unfounded anxieties created for self-protection. Those fears were once a plan to create a comfortable place for their thoughts and feelings. As you grow up you may be barely aware they exist as the walls you created to protect yourself when your mind was immature. But these inhibitions become a burden when we grow up and it's not easy to take them down. When we look for liberation from our inhibitions in drugs we free them for a little while but we reinforce them by believing in them.

Downhill with Drugs

There are dangers to going through life stoned. Being out of touch with reality is like stealing from yourself. Even if drugs help you hide from your problems, there's still a price. It's normal to be confused about your feelings. But drugs don't let you have any feelings. So you may lose faith in your ability to do anything about it, no matter how sincere you are. You know the danger in drugs but any relief might seem worth the risk. Don't forget that some people don't survive their drug experience. That's not an exaggeration. Overdoses, accidents, and a lawless culture prove that drugs can kill you.

Drugs can lead you down a self-destructive spiral. Over time, your ability to take care of yourself can deteriorate. And these powerful chemicals have side effects that can affect your physical health. You might not think about eating well and poor nutrition can strain your body. You might stop caring about yourself and ignore your personal hygiene. Our physical selves can stop being important since all we've been trying to do is make ourselves disappear. The only important thing is relief from our anguish.

IT'S NOT FREE.

The need for money can lead honest people to desperate actions when they see drugs as their means of survival. They might look for an easy way to get money for drugs as well as the basic needs their life demands. So crime becomes a desperate choice for someone with a confused mind and emotional pain. And desperation can easily overcome the revulsion stealing has to our normal humanity. Crime is for people who've given up hope. And who don't look for help when they can't help themselves.

When you're in that much pain the threat of jail probably doesn't matter anymore. And you won't consider the time wasted facing the justice system when you're arrested. Whatever the policies of a community's justice system are, when you break the law it's expensive to fix. It takes your time, money, effort, and reputation. In a worst case scenario it can follow you the rest of your life. Long after you've outgrown your youthful mistakes it can sneak up on you. You might need a license to get a job someday but when your criminal past comes up it could be harder to get.

Don't Go There. It's a Trap!

You might feel you can't handle your problems but with drugs you can control yourself. So drugs become your crutch. But like a crutch used beyond its recuperative benefit it can rob you of your ability to build yourself up. Your healthy parts become weak from disuse as you depend more on the crutch. And unless you choose to cross the bridge from hardship to health you can become dependent on drugs.

Freeing yourself from an addiction can be extremely difficult both psychologically and physically. It's like the pain of exercising a weak muscle back to health. Since it hurts we avoid it. Your body accustoms itself to living with these foreign substances as a part of its nature. So once addicted, eliminating the drugs from your system can be physically painful. But learning what to do to get healthy and then deciding to be healthy are the mountains you have to climb to get over an addiction.

The sad irony is that what had started as something you took for relief instead leaves you suffering being without it. You're trapped; uncomfortable with your problems, uncomfortable being drugged, and unable to stop taking the drugs. Addiction strains the psyche and you can lose yourself in finding relief only by taking more of the one thing you don't want to take at all. Addiction reverses nature. It confines you to an unnatural state where your balance only comes from the influence of drugs.

IT'S NOT JUST DRUGS

There are all kinds of things people crave for emotional comfort. An addiction imitates a tangible purpose when a person's true purpose is unclear. An addiction starts to make sense when nothing else does. It's the increased importance we give to anything that gives us comfort. It's something to cling to when we don't realize it's faith in God that releases us from life's limitations.

We can indulge ourselves with food or entertainment. We can get lost in work or buying things. It could be a fascination with celebrities or an obsession for someone you see every day. It can be sex, money, or the desire to be popular. These can all be harmless fun. They can be interesting and exciting. But when you become attached to something as a reason for living beyond common sense it becomes an addiction and a danger to your freedom.

There are all kinds of addictions. Any habit that replaces your power to reason is an addiction. Anything we look to for comfort before we seek God's guidance is an addiction. Anything we prize before we honor God's power is an addiction. Some people even get addicted to bad relationships. They get stuck in the structure of a familiar pattern no matter how problematic it is. To avoid responsibilities we fear even more, we sometimes attach ourselves to the familiar struggle of a bad job, a bad friend, or a bad lover just because we feel secure in knowing where we are. Though we know it's wrong, we adapt to it and accept our frustrations regardless of our misplaced commitment.

A Soul on Drugs

Misusing drugs can create a barrier in a person's soul that suppresses their will to work. And creativity, our natural connection to God, can stall. Sure, without inhibitions sometimes hidden parts of your personality wonderfully reveal themselves. But those are more like a flash of lightning than the steady glow of your soul's true self. When you accept who you are you have the brilliance of love's wisdom whenever you want.

IT'S NOT JUST DRUGS (continued)

In our search for identity, addiction's no sanctuary. Do you think if something directs you you're not responsible for your life anymore? Do you think if you serve some superior, whose name is whatever dependency you've chosen, you're acting responsibly? NO! It's irresponsibility. Dependency is the choice to retreat. You fool yourself into believing that by giving your free will to the demands of an addiction you're successful by serving that addiction. But when you cut off life's complexities with a dependency you delay your empowerment. An addiction limits your experiences while real success is being able to change things when you want to.

People want to know who they are. Our identities separate our individuality from the background of life. It's partly the truth and partly what we want it to be. That's the work of being alive. People are supposed to make decisions on what's important to them. But it's easy to miss the soul's purpose and get lost in the details. We often get caught up in it and let the details determine our values. You have to accept that you're perfectly okay as you are. When you measure self-worth from one point of view it holds you back from the glory of life's complexity. Psychological addictions are any preoccupation that separates you from your soul's dream. Anything you let be your identity, other than your heart's desire, has the same potential as a physical addiction to force you off your true path.

Even more insidious, when you take drugs you waste your time. Our sense of ourselves changes as we develop our skills for molding the world. That's your responsibility. And it's a great way to spend your time. Even if you don't educate yourself you learn a lot just by experience. But drugs take away your desire for what life offers besides the drugs. Self-reliance is a spirit's goal. And relying on your spirit to give you what you want is what life's all about. The key to finding it is an awareness unburdened by the blur of drugs and alcohol.

The Alternative: Meeting Your Challenges

You have to accept you can deal with your problems without the security you find in drugs. It's hard to face your problems but you'll do infinitely better if you try. It's a common problem. And there's help.

More important you'll regain reuse of your time. You'll be productive again. Life will be your choice again. You can use your time to educate yourself or learn new skills. You can use your time to do your art. And you can use your time to heal yourself and build your future when you have the courage to face down your demons and accept life for what it is.

Life's a challenge for everyone. And no one can handle all life's problems by themselves. It's normal to need help. There's no shame in it. And it's important to ask for help when you do need it. Life will never give you more than you can handle. Life was created to serve you, not defeat you. We all need help. Remember, God's grace protects you. Even at your lowest point, the power of the universe waits for your directions. And this limitless strength empowers every human being—even through the darkest times.

You always have an opportunity to grow through your challenges and find peace with yourself. You can always recover the vision of what's important to you, make the right changes, and get back on the road to success. You might not be there yet. But obstacles should be acknowledged if you want to be self-reliant. Decide to work at it till you win, and you will win! You're designed to be successful.

LYiNG

What is it about lying that affects our human consciousness with such dramatic impact that it reaches to the core of our feelings? Why's the truth so important to us? Why should it make any difference? The reality is people believe what you tell them. It's natural for us to trust each other. We have to work at being distrustful. Human culture is connected and people's experiences are shared. So we trust each other. Truthfulness is part of our agreement to live together peaceably. That's why we find lying so repulsive. We trust our friends. And life shows us there's a place where we can all be friends. But lies betray that friendship. And they distort the potential we have when we work together.

It Happens Every Day.

That's why advertising's so powerful. It's also why we've created "truth in advertising" laws. We know the potential for abuse in promises from strangers. We don't want to be fooled when we believe something someone's told us isn't true. Experience and common sense warn us when there's an obvious reason for lying. But usually our first response is to believe what's said. It's convenient to communication. Different points of consciousness trade information. Then each of us values it according to our plans. So we're constantly subjected to people promoting their perspectives while they look for kindred spirits. And until we know otherwise we tend to believe them. Life's easier when we trust each other.

Lying and dishonesty are part of life. We accept it. But we've created ways to talk about it that justify how much lying we'll tolerate. Knowing that people have their motives and may seek an advantage we take our news "with a grain of salt." We're so intimate with it that we've softened our vocabulary to make it more sociable. We have "spin" for politicians, "artistic license" for writers, and "puffing" for salespeople. So lying doesn't seem so bad. It's almost cute.

IT'S KIND OF A LIE

Lies come in all shapes and sizes. We call them "fibs", "little white lies", and "whoppers" when they're harmless. But a treacherous intent makes them very different. As *obfuscations* they present confusing ideas to fool a believer into missing what's really important. Or as *deceptions* they disguise the truth within the believer's normal inclinations. As *omissions* they leave out critical information so the truth appears differently than what it is.

But the tactics of lying are irrelevant to the harm they do. The size of a lie isn't how far it is from the truth. It's better measured by the damage done by its result. When you're defamed or cheated by someone who's told a "dirty rotten lie" then it's a big lie. There's even a term "big lie" that refers to something said so often that it diminishes the truth to the point of replacing it.

Early on children see the safety in lying to avoid blame. It's such a natural convenience that they have to be corrected to stop doing it. They have to learn the social cost in the loss of trust that comes with the fragile security in a lie. So kids grow up with conflicting guidance. In the schoolyard they learn, "liar, liar, pants on fire." and that "crying wolf" is a terrible thing to do. But they also learned that a good lie, like a "tall tale", can be entertaining. Or that guessing the best liar on some game show could be fun. Whether a lie means betrayal and injustice or just some innocent fun is for you to decide. Anyway, lying is a part of us.

There's another side too. "Are you calling me a liar?" is an instant challenge to fight. It's one of the most awful insults that can be said about someone. It's a strange phenomenon. Lying is more or less accepted but being accused of being a liar is one of the worst things that could be said about a person's character. The emotional pain comes from our souls because honesty is the heart of reality. Every moment we seek the meaning of our lives. So we revere the truth.

Just Words?

Words are the world for lies. What makes words tricky is that even a small difference can change their meaning. A change in tone or adding a qualifier makes it easy to "say one thing and mean another." Lawyers know it and create documents so confusing that it takes another lawyer to interpret them. Even then lawyers can disagree on what the language actually says. And every word in a legal document is important even if it's confusing. If you agree to its terms, whether it's clear or not, you'll be held accountable to it.

Asking for what you want isn't wrong. But if the details of who's responsible for what are buried in a mountain of "legalese" you should respect yourself and question the document's fairness. Honest intentions should be openly expressed. You can protect your interests, be complete and foresighted, and still state your case simply. True, it's possible the language is needed to clarify the agreement and avoid future problems. But it's weird how the creation can be so baffling when the intent is to create an understanding. For those people "good for their word" an agreement can be as easy as a handshake. But however you make your agreements you should always protect yourself against dishonesty.

Written agreements can be confusing. So it's a good idea to question any contract you sign. Whether you're buying a car, renting an apartment, or doing some business, read what you're signing. If someone's impatient or objects, you can be sure they're thinking about themselves and not you.

It's true. Reading a contract takes time. And it's inconvenient. But like brushing your teeth, it's part of the job of living and the natural course of taking care of yourself. Remember, you can take a contract home and read it at your own pace without troubling anyone. Or you can have someone you trust read it for you. Sometimes a schedule demands that you make your decision right away. But there's no choice you'll ever have to make that requires your signature where you won't have time to read it and know what you're signing.

Just Be Honest With Yourself.

There's a saying, "To thine own self be true." It means more than being your own best friend. It means it's important to be honest with yourself. In your thoughts you should think of yourself truthfully. You can appreciate your abilities without thinking you're better than anyone else. And you can accept your faults without feeling that you're less than anyone else.

As life would have it, honesty and accuracy can be far apart. You could be wrong in your understanding but your desire should be to always face the truth—whatever it is. It's because you can work with the truth. When you know the facts you can exploit the good things for your benefit. And you can change the things you don't like to become the person you do like. You can see yourself as the person you want to be and not someone people expect you to be.

Lying to yourself wastes your time. Lies only delay the inevitable. The truth, like justice, is perfect and complete. God's accounting for it is specific and eternal. The truth will always resolve itself. When you're "fooling yourself" you're solving nonexistent problems. But on your "true path" you accept yourself without judgment for being the person you are. When you're honest you can love every part of yourself and still appreciate there can be room for improvement. With time and the truth you can heal your character and become the person you really are—the one you enjoy and admire.

Why We Lie

People tell lies for different reasons. Sometimes they lie for convenience. It's easier for them to "tell a lie" than have to explain the truth. Lying can be innocent and without malice. Sometimes you'd rather tell a "little lie" than say something which might hurt someone's feelings. For example, you might know someone who wants a relationship with you but you're really not interested. So when they ask if you want to get together you tell them you've already made plans. Hopefully they'll take the hint and understand that, for whatever reason, you don't want to be friendly with them. You're not obligated to be friends with anyone you don't want to. But you can appreciate their kindness. So out of respect for their feelings you lie.

When someone's having a bad time you might tell them everything's okay because you don't want them to be discouraged. Families tell loved ones everything's okay, even when it's not, so they won't worry about them. Someone may want to help you but you say you don't need any help because you don't want to burden them. You think it'd be unfair. You can love and respect someone yet mislead them because sometimes it's more generous to lie.

The Lies We Love

Some lies are tolerated just because we like them. It's fun to hear outrageous "stories" whose innocent intent is to share imagination's wonders. "Spinning yarns" about unbelievable circumstances fascinate

THE UNFAIRNESS IN FRAUD

A hoax becomes a fraud when the intention of the deceiver is to create an advantage. In a fraud the liar intends to trick the believer into accepting a lie as equal value for what's traded for it.

- It's intentionally selling a "fake" work of art as a valuable original.
- It's knowingly offering investments in worthless companies.
- It's charging for work never intended to be done or for products never meant to be delivered.
- It's tricking someone into believing they have a problem, when they don't, to fool them into paying for something they don't need.

A fraud profits from someone's misplaced trust. The payoff is usually financial but it can be anything the lie achieves. Institutionalized by criminals it takes the form of a "con game." But it fascinates us as movies like *"The Sting"* and *"The Grifters"* romanticize its allure of easy money and a carefree life.

The history of fraud reaches from the "Trojan Horse" of ancient history to the "Trojan Horse Computer Viruses" we deal with today. Now we have "police stings" where crooks are tricked into committing their crimes where they can be taped for the proof that convicts them in court. Law enforcement "police decoys" are even used to attract crime. Then the fraud is a way to get criminals off the street and we accept it.

us. We tell kids about the "Easter Bunny" and the "Tooth Fairy." Everyone loves it so it's fun. Because whatever's done in a loving spirit honestly opens our souls.

Then again some people are just gullible. Even when it's nonsense they'll believe whatever you tell them. With "wild stories" we amaze ourselves how some people have no limits to what they'll believe. "They'll believe anything."

We've even created a holiday to celebrate lying and make each other feel stupid. Since we were children we've looked forward to "April Fool's Day." Then we could "play a trick" on someone who'd want to be part of the fun. It's a chance to laugh at ourselves. And it brings us back to reality when we realize we're still part of nature.

We have fun with "hoaxes" too. A hoax can be clever and funny. It's usually something so "far-fetched" that only a "chump" would believe it. A hoax could be faking "Bigfoot" tracks in the woods then enjoying the excitement watching people argue over it. Real or not, it's sure unusual and worth looking at. It's because harmlessness makes a hoax. But there's a point where a hoax crosses the line of innocence and intentionally hurts people. Then it's a fraud.

And Nothing But the Truth

At the other end of the spectrum is our unqualified respect for telling the truth in court. Telling the truth in court is essential because only in the truth can we find real justice. Our courts represent social order and equal treatment for all members of society. So fairness depends on an accurate presentation of the facts so everyone gets what's rightly theirs and pays what they rightly owe. It's so important that we've made it a crime to lie in court. It's "perjury" and a person can go to jail if they're convicted of it.

But it balances on a strange philosophy. One view is that telling the truth in court is almost sacred. More than a crime against society, to "perjure yourself" is considered a sacrilege—a crime against God. And that by "swearing in" you've agreed to "tell the truth, the whole truth, and nothing but the truth, so help you God."

But I believe people are always "under oath"—with no ceremony needed. When I talk to anyone I expect them to be truthful. I know they could be lying but an oath won't help. A lie is the same whether a person gives their oath or not. It may be a rule of the judicial process but the absence of an oath doesn't exempt anyone from their responsibility to tell the truth.

An oath is ceremonial but that doesn't diminish its importance. Ceremonies have meaning. An oath is a public statement of the intention to tell the truth no matter what the result may be. It's power for the one who takes an oath because it adds value to their words. And it's reassurance to those who rely on the implicit trust in an oath because they might do something for the sole reason that someone "took an oath." But even if an oath tricks someone into believing a lie, it only reinforces the belief. It doesn't affect the truth at all.

It's Part of the Game.

We prize deception in competition. We love when our team "fakes out" an opponent and scores. Or we pretend we're sick and hurting when we're really strong and fit to "fool" the other side into being careless. Sometimes we pretend we're stronger than we really are to intimidate an opponent into playing badly. Likewise in business we use "gamesmanship" to pretend we're doing one thing while we "secretly" do something else. We want to "outsmart" our competitors and have a better chance of winning. Like an animal's natural camouflage in its environment, lying is a part of the human game.

Another Lying Politician

We expect lies from politicians. It's a sad joke we accept. We say they're "playing politics." And that "mischief" and "dirty tricks" are just part of the process. We expect that people will "say anything to get elected." We have doubts about "campaign promises" but we "look the other way" and accept it as "just politics."

In politics there are lies about facts, lies about policies, and lies about people. The truth is often "swept under the rug", "out of sight, out of mind." Hiding a politician's bad reputation improves it "in the public eye" while another politician's reputation is "smeared" by misrepresenting their record.

A lie may be quickly forgotten but its result can continue on as an unfair policy. Then the public must live with that lie while the politicians keep trying to be "everything to everybody." Politicians live in their "public image" and it's open to scrutiny. So they try to create the "perception" that appeals to the most voters.

Politicians often disdain the public and treat them as incidental to their ambitions. They trust the publicity, not the public. They equate publicity with believability. They believe the public has "a short memory" for a politico's shortcomings. They think they can dodge it or tell another lie. And the media too, with all their political views, see any rumor of scandal as sufficient opportunity to present allegations regardless of the facts. If something's exciting and defensible in court they'll shout it out as loud and often as they can. Interest is good for business whether you're selling ads or policies. In that way politics is like sports. It's a competition over who should be believed.

There's another kind of lie in politics...corruption! The "public trust" has every citizen being treated fairly without favoritism. And a community is betrayed when a public official's main concern is their own enrichment. Secret payments and hidden benefits are a lie to the community.

Public officials are the communal extension of our personal responsibilities. So we demand the truth from them. But there are times when the truth creates a conflict for a politician, especially when people disagree with them. Sometimes lives hang in the balance and the outcome is more important than the truth. Sometimes there's no time for debate, and revealing the truth could cause greater problems. Sometimes telling the truth is the wrong thing to do. But lying should always be taken seriously. There should be an overriding selfless necessity before you lie to someone who's delegated their trust to you. And you're responsible for what you do even if no one else ever knows. Lies may damage a liar. It focuses on the opinion someone has about themselves. God knows the truth. So a person's intentions matter. The question is whether a person can justify sacrificing their integrity to the truth in their conscience. Just know that if you're ever confronted with this kind of conflict, sincerity is in your desire to do the right thing.

What Did You Expect?

There's no end to lying and it comes in many forms. There's a saying that "The first casualty of war is the truth." We accept "disinformation" because lying for our security protects us. Lying and dishonesty as character flaws seem a small price to pay when our freedom's threatened. Then a lie, like "camouflage", supports our survival.

Making war is the most extreme expression of any society. It's the willingness to risk everything. War, or even a threat, is all it takes to suspend our normal behavior. Our values are revised to meet the threat. Then lying can become a tool of policy. "Propaganda" sells a single point of view to advance the cause. Spies "spread lies" to confuse the enemy. And "ruses" are devised to mislead the foe. So lying becomes a weapon.

It's common knowledge that people lie about money. Everyone knows the joke about "Honest John's Used Cars." He's the last person you'd believe about anything let alone trust what he says about a used car you're buying. With fraudulent financial practices the offender might "candy coat" them, calling them "aggressive accounting." They "justify one lie with another" so it appears they haven't done anything wrong. And "puffing", something a salesperson says to make a deal look better, is understood to be less than the truth but not quite a lie. They can't misrepresent the facts but they can let their enthusiasm overstate the value of what they're selling.

Lawyers regularly describe things as "the worst they've ever seen" or "Everyone knows it's true." They use extreme language to convince a jury when they're really too smart to believe that any situation exists in a vacuum of absolutes. Then they emphatically repeat the exaggeration to reinforce its believability. They try to transfer the power of their belief to the listener. So "stretching the truth" is accepted as part of the process when important matters are argued.

In every business, regardless of the handshakes and smiles, everyone knows there's a "hidden agenda." That agenda is money. Like everything in life there are problems in doing business. So inventory shortages get blamed on the weather. Or manufacturing problems are blamed on the poor soul who was just fired yesterday. To maintain harmony with customers, lies are often used as convenient appeasements. Where's the order? "Your order's on the truck." is the answer to shipping delays. Where's the payment? "The check is in the mail." is the answer to overdue invoices. Business lying is a survival tactic for dealing with problems beyond anyone's control. If the intention is fair and honest and neither fraudulent nor mercenary, a business person may resort to "half-truths" as long as they can avoid offending someone and continue a respectful relationship. Problems in business are expected. So to be sure that everyone gets what they agreed to, "Don't believe the hype." and "Always get it in writing!"

The Best Policy

"Telling lies" to people we know is part of everyday life. It can be innocent or treacherous. Though inconsiderate, a lot of people don't care because it's so easy to do. Children tell "fibs." Spouses tell "cheating lies." And people taking undue credit or making unfair accusations feed the "gossip mill" at work. So we're accustomed to lying. Whether it's "double-talk" or "with forked tongue", it's part of the human experience. It's the way we hide behind words and the false images they create.

But we live with the lies we tell. It becomes part of our character and we're responsible for them. Some people "live a lie" while others have faith in the truth. And it's you who chooses the value you give to being honest.

In a world of "habitual liars", "pathological liars", and now "serial liars", it's comforting to remember that George Washington, a founding father of our country, "never told a lie." We admire his honesty. The legend says he admitted "chopping down the cherry tree." In grade school we were taught though he acknowledged felling the tree he still took pride in his honesty. "I cannot tell a lie." was his statement of courage and faith. It's hopeful for us that we revere this story. It's comforting how we teach it to our children as an example of good character. That such a great person should so much prize the truth, and that it reflects our values today, is good reason to have hope for our future. So have faith in the truth. After all, "Honesty is the best policy."

Family Values

There's a lot of flag-waving that goes with raising the banner of "family values." Self-serving politicians find a political issue in the love family members have for each other. It's an old idea. It's just a new name for a well-worn political tactic. It used to be called "mom, the flag, and apple pie." It's effective because it touches our instinct for survival. We cheer for the strength and intimacy in a family's love. And we cherish our nation's traditions. They show us our goodness. So we appreciate the opportunities they give us.

Then what could ever threaten this abundance? Certainly, arrogant politicians are ready to tell us. They frighten us with rhetoric of a nation's failed character to create the public fear that empowers their ambitions. They wrap themselves in gaudy righteousness instead of exemplifying right action. Lots of things can be improved and there are plenty of opportunities for people with loving hearts to change things for the better. But abusing people's feelings by "crying wolf" and inciting people to thoughtless action is a shame.

There are true "family values" unique to the soul of human values all people cherish. Since politicians rarely address real family values, they're either out of touch with how important they are or they're afraid of them. In fact, the expression of family values is so intimate that politicians avoid the real issues because they don't want to offend anyone. That's why family values are rarely explained. The rallying cry of "family values" is an easier way to excite people. As if one political point of view had more insight on love than the other.

Family values aren't political, cultural, or religious values. They're more than that. True family values are about the quality of life that comes from God. They're *family of humanity values*. They're the positive social values we share as human beings living on this plane in common knowledge of our spiritual nature.

The Real Values

Family values begin with the special love between a parent and child. The intensity of this love can't be fairly described. It has to be experienced to be fully appreciated. In being a parent is the opportunity to have a little of life's indescribable mystery explained. It's a peek at the power of God's love. In the name of this love parents have made legendary sacrifices for their children. With little concern for their own safety and only the thought to protect the ones they love, parents have jumped into frozen lakes, run into burning buildings, and confronted murderous thugs. Disregarding their own comfort, a parent's love can take them to go to war or work two jobs. Some would sacrifice everything they have for a family member and never think it a hardship. They see it as an act of love for the person they're helping.

Healthy families see helping each other as an opportunity, not an obligation. It's a joy for them and they're grateful to share it. At Boy's Town in Omaha, Nebraska there's a statue of a boy carrying another boy piggyback on his shoulders. Inscribed on its base is the answer to a question asked by Father Flanagan, the creator of Boy's Town, about the younger boy being too much to carry. The answer from the older boy was simple and heartfelt—"He ain't heavy, father. He's m' brother." So, blessed by God, a family's love can defy Earth's limitations.

A family's intimacy is unlike anything else in life. Unfortunately, all parent/child relationships are not happy experiences. But whether or not it's appreciated, a family's opportunity to create love is unique.

Its potential lies in the traditional way it lovingly joins people to their network of support. A family teaches each new member how to contribute to the family. Each one helps the other and they all share the satisfaction in each one's success. Much of the love a person creates in life comes directly from their family.

Family values are about the opportunities love has to increase itself. We can see it in the love we share with our siblings. Coming from a common experience gives us a bond. It's a shared upbringing—loving the same people and sharing the same circumstances. Helping and caring for each other make a family. Sometimes a family's best friends are given the honorary titles of "Aunt" and "Uncle." And a family is modeled where membership demonstrates its commitment by calling each other "brother" or "sister" like you might find in a religious group or trade union. It means they support each other. Family values are about appreciating love and accomplishment beyond yourself. And a loving family can be fertile ground for developing the positive outlook that helps you meet life's challenges.

Healthy families stand up for each other. Through life's tragedies—failed careers, failed marriages, failed health, or failed character—no lost cause is beyond their concern. During Argentina's "Dirty War", between 1976 and 1983, people were kidnapped by the government and never heard from again. Their families weren't even told what had happened. But the mothers of those abducted never gave up hope. Every day they'd meet at the government buildings and stand in protest. They lived a tireless love for their missing children. It's true they probably knew their children had been murdered. But they wouldn't give up hope till it was proved beyond a doubt. Still they wanted their children's bodies returned. If they couldn't love them in life, at least they would honor them in loving memory.

The family connection and the value of each family member is the meaning of family values. It goes beyond religious and cultural values. It's a human value. And it's part of life everywhere. From the deserts of Africa to the jungles of South America, from the industrialized cities of Europe to the suburbs of America, families love, teach, help, and encourage themselves through their love for each other. It's basic to our being. A family helps itself by helping its members. And the members help themselves by supporting the family. It's the primary human relationship and whether or not it succeeds it has the potential to be the most supportive experience in the life of its participants.

FAMILIES HAVE PROBLEMS TOO

Of course that's a positive look at a family's potential. It by no means ignores the struggles of families who can't co-operate together or who face problems beyond their abilities. Life can be hard to understand at any age and the capabilities we're given to deal with it may be limited. And sometimes family support just isn't there.

Life's pressures can fatigue a family to the point that it's more than they can endure. And a family can break apart. Or family members can lose their connection and get lost in life's diversions. Some people don't see the opportunity in family membership. They never see themselves as part of a team. They sadly believe a family's value just isn't worth the effort.

But even in the worst situations there's a compelling bond in a shared experience. Sometimes the vision of a family is more in spirit than the guarantee of a happy ending. But whether it's cherished or reviled, the potential to create love in these unique relationships is a commitment designed by God.

The Human Family

Humanity grows through mutual support. Life's an abundant experience and we gain the most when we help each other see that. The human family can surmount great challenges. Its variety helps it adapt to many situations. So, new experiences can be explored. And we can understand it because we're all relatives. We love each other. We never blame people for the conflicts between nations; we blame their unreasonable governments. People get along fine when you let them. Cooperation does start somewhere though. It's in the quality of our family relationships that we introduce ourselves to the greater relationships of society. So with a positive outlook, the world prospers and the human family does well.

Appreciating Each Other

Families go through stages and teen responsibilities can be intense. You're a young adult now. Your outlook and desires are developed but you're still trying to figure out what you want and how to get it. It's normal. It's the part of life that comes with being young. Though hard to accept, you just have to give it time. And unless controlled, impatience can strike out in rebellion against authority. That includes your family. You may want to fight against the family limits holding you back when it's really the predicament of growing up that's the enemy. And the enemy can't be defeated. So it must be embraced. It's the family's job to help you through this challenging time. If you reject the steps maturity requires from you, you may grow up feeling incomplete. If you rely just on yourself you may wind up frightened and frustrated by this predictable struggle. It's hard but it's normal and it passes. And you grow through it like everyone else.

Remember, the family bond is created through love and caring. Family love is epitomized in the wisdom to "Honor thy mother and father." A child might not know much but they know where to go for help. So honoring our parents means respecting the advice they lovingly offer. It means paying attention to someone's concerns about you. But that responsibility isn't only carried by the children. A parent or family member who gives advice bears the same responsibility. They must honor the trust as well. So advice should be fair. It should respect what everyone wants. The real guidance should be, "Honor your mother and father, and honor your children too."

This period in life is a benchmark for your experiences throughout the course of your lifetime. And the spirit of your generation, with its shared experiences, will stay with you the rest of your life. But a family shares its generational differences with its new adults. Modern attitudes don't matter. The change is always the same. Adult family members have already gone through the phase you're going through now. And they've asked the same questions you're asking now. And they found answers. And they formed their opinions. And through the benefits of time and experience they've refined their opinions into an understanding of how life works. So your family still offers credible insights that can help you meet contemporary challenges with foresight and confidence.

Teen Angst

We used to think teen rebellion was some bored teenagers breaking into school overnight and knocking over some desks. And it was always the "bad kids" who got blamed for it. Today the rebellion's the same but it has a new demeanor. Now we suffer the horrors of mass violence as unbridled freedom and the endless access to raw knowledge reach out to even the youngest members of society. Kids grow up faster today because they're exposed to more mature subjects at a younger age. There are some things young people can handle well by themselves and other things they can do well with adult supervision. But there are some things they can't handle well at all. For those things they have to be patient and wait to gain some experience.

Out of the Mouths of Babes

The family is a guide. And any member at any age has the opportunity to improve themselves by it. The spiral of maturity feeds from a family's wealth of experience. What might take you years to learn, someone else in the family already knows. And a family shares its lessons. A wife shares her insights with her husband. An older sibling shares the day's discoveries with their brothers and sisters. And parents teach their children that whatever the direction it's the same path for everyone. A loving family is the gentlest introduction to life ever devised. It's the amazing mechanism God's created to help us as we develop self-reliance.

A New Generation

New ideas percolate through a culture and stimulate open young minds. It's youth's nature to look for exciting new experiences. And they find them too. But they're not limited to exploring a known world only new to them. They can explore anything that's possible and invent what they don't find. But newness like any unknown may have dangers. The generation of the 1960's experimented with drugs in its search for love but with that understanding they learned the burden of drug addiction too. The generation of the 1980's developed a high standard of living but with their success came the imbalanced materialism of the "Me Generation."

It's in situations like these where the miracle of a family becomes a counterweight and brings balance to the new generation's plans. The family is a safety line to the wisdom of past generations. The amazing thing is how well families adapt to solving problems that were never even imagined.

For Generations to Come

A family's love is timeless. It can last a lifetime for the care of an invalid relative or go beyond death in the loving commemoration of visits to the cemetery to remember a loved one who's passed. A family knows that when the pain of disappointment passes the gentle memories of love remain. The love continues. The value in a family is that each generation can pick up and pass along the torch of the family's strength and with it enduring opportunities for its future generations. A family's power is built up in layers of tribulation and achievement. And it's built on again and again. That's why a family's integrity is important and worth supporting.

HEROES, CELEBRITIES, & ROLE MODELS

My Hero

Who we want to be depends a lot on who we use as an example. So we look for heroes to show us the right way to live. There's no question how important heroism is to the human condition. It takes a brave person to make a conscious sacrifice for someone else. And life demands that we all be brave. It's the greatest expression of faith that we have on our planet.

We give our heroes more respect than we give anyone else. We declare holidays in their honor and celebrate their heroic acts with ceremonies and parades. Rightly so, we appreciate them protecting us. They stand up when the odds of victory are against them but the rightness of their purpose compels them to challenge the danger.

A hero is anyone who takes themselves from a place of safety or comfort into a situation of danger or hardship for the sake of someone else. It's unusual due to the conflict we have between self-preservation and the love we feel for someone in need. It's the greatest act of love a person can do. Heroes willingly endanger themselves and all they are to aid someone, often a stranger, who needs their help.

Heroism is available to anyone but for most it's coincidence. It's not the kind of thing people plan on doing. Just the opposite, we usually make plans to avoid dangerous situations. This gift from our heroes helps us to personalize courage and understand the right thing to do when we're confronted by the stress of a dangerous situation. It's because we're so conscious of our safety that the actions of a hero are exceptional.

It's important to remember that personal courage goes beyond physical safety. Sometimes being a hero means speaking up for your beliefs even when they clash with the community's thinking. A hero who openly shares their beliefs risks being ridiculed or, even worse, having to confront the society's legal system and its perils. A hero's ideas can threaten a community as much as their physical courage ever could. And often a community will fight new ideas as hard as they'd fight off any foreign attack. But the "courage of your convictions" shows bravery. Your courage trusts that when the truth is realized, the false beliefs will fall aside.

Some people choose careers that increase the possibility they'll test their courage. Those who join the police, fire department, or military can expect to encounter dangerous situations in their daily routine. While there's excitement and challenge in these professions, there's also a unique opportunity to provide service to the community. For this good reason these people have always been considered our heroes. They're real heroes. Their daily job is to resolve dangerous situations safely and consider their own safety secondary.

Celebrity in the Media Age

In contrast to heroes, celebrities are artificial creations. They're intentionally created by themselves, their agents, or the media. It's simple marketing. The person becomes a product. They're selling their personalities. Celebrities exploit the media to increase their public profile so they can make money, aggrandize themselves, or promote a cause. They simply become characters in the stories the media sells to its customers.

For most celebrities, fame lasts as long as there's an effort to keep their image alive in the public eye. It's like a balloon with a picture painted on the outside. As long as there's air inside to give the balloon shape you see the image. But when the pressure's released the balloon deflates and the image disappears. And fame is quickly forgotten as more contemporary idols gain the attention of a new generation.

Be a Role Model

Role models on the other hand are people who've accomplished something extraordinary in life. We admire what they've done. They represent the positive qualities of character and achievement that we desire for ourselves and those we love. A role model could be an athlete who's mixed their natural talent with personal commitment to achieve something great in their sport. Or it could be someone who's overcome an adversity to accomplish their dream. A role model can be anyone—of any age or background—who does something exemplary.

There are extraordinary personalities throughout history who were able to mix their celebrity with being a role model. These saints of celebrity were bigger than the world around them. From Joan of Arc to Elvis Presley we still love and honor them. They epitomized in their human form the ideals we cherish today. They loved the world. And neither the fires of fearful superstitions, the drug fed flames of self-destruction, nor any other part of their humanity could ever take that from them. They were beyond the average person yet one of them. The love the world has

AND THE AWARD GOES TO...

Awards are the way we honor the people we respect for their accomplishments. They're material representations used to spotlight an achievement. It's how we acknowledge ourselves and elevate the values we admire. We single out for recognition the people we feel have excelled at their endeavors. So it's important to remember that an award represents the giver as much as it honors the recipient. Awards represent the qualities prized by that one group. And as that they're a great way for recognizing an achievement publicly.

Where there's competition for an award, realize that picking something as best or better than anything else is practically impossible. It's a decision made by people and people have preferences. Many accomplishments are worthy of praise. And the concept that we give awards is more important than whether a particular person gets one.

for them continues because the way they loved the world was greater than their humanity.

Honoring Ourselves

It's satisfying to be acknowledged for what you've done. We all enjoy the social acceptance in being recognized for our achievements. Social acceptance is a big part of human nature. But social acceptance isn't about how popular you are. The real meaning of social acceptance is having self-respect in your respect for others. Though you may identify yourself by the groups you're in, you're never totally defined by any one group. Eventually each of us must learn to define who we are to ourselves.

CONTROVERSiES: THE CONFLiCT iN DiFFERENCES

So why's there so much conflict in the world? Why's there so much disagreement about what's the right thing to do? You'd think reasonable people would feel the same way about things. And you'd think most people are as reasonable as you. It should be simple. It should be obvious. Mostly we have similar experiences. We all know what it's like to be alive. So we feel for each other. So how can there be all this passion in different points of view when we're looking at the same problems?

For things without consequence the differences are unimportant. *What kind of movies do you like? What's your favorite ice cream? What kind of clothes do you like to wear?* None of these really matter. So it's more important that everyone should respect your point of view and your contribution to society. They should respect the person you are and the possibilities you offer. They should respect your personality. But what happens when a person with an aggressive physical personality gets together with a quiet thoughtful one? How can both enjoy themselves and share the same activities without limiting each other? The answer is it's not possible. There have to be limits. So in social environments there must be compromises.

And you don't need widely divergent lifestyles to find differences. You can have different opinions on everyday issues with people just like yourself. Something could be important to you but mean very little to someone else. Or you might not care as much about something that affects you both. Some things are personal preferences. But in society these differences decide what's right or wrong for a person's conduct. And that matters to everyone.

MORALS

So what do you think is morally right? How do you feel about it? Morality examines our responsibilities with respect to our ability. Within that, it's how you believe people should act towards each other. It's the physical face of how we love each other. It's good conduct and manners. It's what you expect for others because you expect the same thing for yourself. It's fairness. Morals are human values which respect the limitations, responsibilities, and consequences each of us must face.

Then who's right?

People on any side of an issue can feel they have the moral high ground. They may fervently believe righteousness blesses them while it curses all others. And they'll have their faith and honesty to support them. They'll have studies with statistics for evidence. And they'll have heartfelt testimonials that prove their point. But where justice is the question, what's right is usually somewhere in between.

It's a balance of opposing views. The challenge is how to make the compromises fair to all perspectives.

And it's a tough choice when every time you weigh the facts by a different value the outcome changes. Sometimes there's no clear choice. It's not as simple a question as whether to leave a burning building to save your life. Benefits and costs must be compared to how they're shared. And there are always unanswered questions that obscure the future. So it's a challenging responsibility that affects other people.

It's Your Choice.

But there are times you have to make decisions. It's your right and you deserve it. You just have to realize that making a decision can be hard for anyone. There's going to be winners and losers. But you'll have to think things through the best you can and either do something or not. Whatever you decide, you should take positions on issues. It's important for you to be a conscious member of society. Remember, you're not locked in to anything forever. You can always change your mind. But you have to accept your beliefs to respect yourself. We all want to do the right thing. So morality should be flexible enough to serve our changing needs. Because, whatever the balance, fairness stays the same.

It Happens Every Day.

In a practical way your opinion directly affects your life. Your point of view determines how you spend your money and how you'll accept your taxes being spent. More important is that your decisions affect the rights of others. And their decisions affect you. So how do we set limits that are fair to everyone? What will be required from you that you didn't choose? And how will the compromises have equal value and at the same time promote a social order that's acceptable to everyone?

The challenge of civilization is to bring opposite sides together for everyone's benefit. It's in negotiating compromises that everyone respects. So think about the following issues. You'll be confronting them one way or another for the rest of your life. Then form your opinions and decide for yourself what's right.

Abortion: This extremely emotional issue goes to the heart of people's beliefs about where human experience begins and the value of human life. Those against abortion have the opinion that a fetus, or even an embryo, is a child and that abortions murder children. Those who support the right to have an abortion have the opinion that a fetus is not a child but is instead a part of a woman's personal experience. And that having an abortion should be considered her choice. The reason it's such an intense conflict is that both sides are right, and they're right for the right reasons.

Adoption: Adoption serves for the care of a child to help someone who's unable to care for that child themselves. And it can be a blessing on everyone involved. But because it's so intimate, emotionally charged issues come up. First, there's the person adopted and their mixed feelings about being given up to be raised by someone other than their birth parents. Then there's the parent who gave their child up for adoption, leaving them alone to an uncertain future. And there may be a problem after years of separation where a reunion's desired between the birth parent and child to help them in understanding their lives. There can be a conflict if only one of the biological relations desires it. Or legal obstacles may frustrate a natural parent's and grown child's desire to meet.

Advertising: Is it a simple offer or manipulation? Here the question is about the power of the media and its honest presentation of the facts. Simple signs and shouted offers have evolved into "junk mail" and a constant blare of electronic "drumming" supported by professional studies of human behavior. So you have to question if an ad is a fair appeal to someone's freedom of choice. Or is it calculated to direct someone to do something by stimulating their subconscious instinct regardless of what they want?

Alien Life in the Universe: Are we alone in the universe or do we share this experience of self-awareness with other conscious beings on far-off worlds? On Earth we can see how life expresses itself in many adaptations. We share this planet with donkeys and daisies and every imaginable life-form. From flying fish to giant redwoods they all experience life within God's mandate. Their shapes and behaviors uniquely serve them. And they possess their life in that uniqueness. But they also share it in the world's systems, from its great oceans to the local pond.

If you think extremes define alien life, you can find it in the most inhospitable places here on Earth. We've learned life can thrive under the enormous pressure at the bottom of the ocean. We see it thrive in parched deserts and the frigid emptiness of the Arctic. It swims and it flies. And it knows its spiritual nature. And if life can grow here on our planet, there's no reason to believe that it couldn't grow somewhere else in the universe too.

The hardest thing to understand is how big the universe is because the distances are so great. Its size is still debated among scientists. It's hard to comprehend because there's no reference point in our daily lives that makes sense in comparison. To measure its size scientists describe its distances in "light-years." That's the distance light travels in a year when it's moving at 186,000 miles per second. And other planets aren't just a couple of light-years away. The distances between stars can be hundreds of thousands of light-years. That's a lot of room for living.

Also consider that there are <u>billions</u> of stars and their planets in galaxies throughout the universe. And the universe is filled with <u>billions</u> of galaxies. And every one is an opportunity for a planet to create favorable conditions for life—even if it's not a life-form familiar to us. And God's consciousness touches them just as easily forming material experiences suitable to expressing creativity and exploring existence.

Earth exists in a relatively rural part of the universe away from the greatest density of stars and planets. That could be the reason we've had just limited contact with other worlds. It's my opinion that it's unlikely Earth's the only place in the universe with life. Instead I believe there are millions of planets in the universe supporting life spiritually conscious of God. And through God we're all alike. Regardless of our physical forms we're all connected in consciousness.

We'll relate to each other from that place in spirit too. And we'll love each other. We want to see their wonders. We often think our life is plain and ignore the wonders we have here already. All science fiction is just a reflection of our everyday life. Take a look. On Earth we have great sand deserts and massive glacial ice fields. We have water falling from the sky. We have rivers of molten rock. We have fire and colors. We have elements and energies and the imagination to mold them. In imagination we share the feast of consciousness. So why do we look to outer space for enlightenment when enlightenment is right outside our door? If you want to explore a new planet, explore your own. All you have to do is reach for it.

That doesn't mean we're not unique to the cause of universal consciousness. We may well be. Earth could be to the universe what Jerusalem means to us here—a spiritual center and worldwide holy place. Advanced technologies don't prove that an alien culture is any more spiritually aware than we are.

And we question the motives of alien visitations in the same way we'd question anyone's motives. We're cautious but optimistic. We have to protect ourselves whatever happens. It doesn't matter if they're new neighbors or someone new at work. We see them all the same way—as *foreigners*. They probably see us the same way too. But differences in cultures present opportunities. In situations where cultures meet there's a chance for learning. Every contact has the excitement of fresh perspectives and intriguing solutions to universal problems.

So where's the proof of alien life? Show me! Without evidence the debate goes on. But it's more a mental exercise and emotional outlet than anything practical. It's like arguing if some old-time sports team could beat your favorite team today. So what! We'll either know someday for sure or we'll keep on wondering. It makes sense though for there to be other conscious beings in the universe. So we explore outer space hoping to meet them someday and understand consciousness from their point of view.

Whether or not we believe aliens exist—like Bigfoot and the Loch Ness Monster—we want them to be real. We like anything new. And we like it a lot if it's a new way of looking at ourselves. That's what we look forward to finding. We want to understand ourselves better in comparison.

Animal Rights: This is part of the evolving understanding of humanity's relationship to the other life-forms that share this planet. Animal rights are about respecting the natural rights of all living things in our ecology. They're about every living thing being able to express the power of its animate expression in balance with the rest of the world. This includes the mineral world. Volcanoes, crystals, and caves have a kind of living expression too. Natural rights include forests as well as flood plains and city parks. But it's normal for diverse natural forces to intrude on their neighbors. So to appreciate life we have to respect the balance between things.

Does any level of biological or ecological organization have a greater right to life than another? Is a microbe less deserving than a dog? All life strives for survival in its own unique way. And we're entitled to our lives too. But despite what human beings want, this planet has its own balance. And it won't tolerate imbalance. No plague or nuclear winter could overcome it. Human beings might not be able to live here but the world will survive. It'll endure any imbalance then reestablish itself in its natural way. The world fulfills its destiny to exist too.

According to our special nature human beings must act on this planet to survive here. But our lives depend on a healthy planet to provide our sustenance. It's our right to claim our portion of this world to express our lives. When we press against its limits we have a home here. But when we retreat, life's imperative takes its turn. And like a lost city in a jungle of overgrowth, new life will replace us.

But when we heed our planet's needs we can exploit it without damaging it. When we respect the balance we have no other limits.

So if we want to flourish here we have to adjust our potential to respect a natural world that goes its own way.

We've exploited this planet in every imaginable way to make our lives better. That's our creative nature. But human beings, as part of the environment, suffer when we're more concerned with convenience than having compassion for our planet. The Earth is *our home*. Whether we live in a mansion or a dilapidated hovel is up to us. The world is our source for success. With technology and a maturing attitude we can replace our shortsighted treatment of the world with an inspired wisdom that respects all life.

Architecture: Do you like it? Do you even care? There's beauty and purpose in architecture because beauty and purpose exist in all things. But architecture offers a unique opportunity—in its details and proportions—to awe us with its creative difficulty. We ask ourselves, "How did they do that?" Size and strength make an impression. And the power to make strength beautiful can inspire or frighten us. It's what you like and how you use it that makes architecture what it is. Whether you find buildings especially important to you is your decision. But it's an odd thing how we enjoy watching them knocked down as much as we like seeing them go up.

Art & Music: Like architecture, art and music come out of human creativity. Their essence is the need human beings have to express their perception of life. We describe our outlook through the raw material of our experience. Then it's sifted through our minds to be made real through skill and inspiration. It's the way we explore consciousness as it reveals an infinite creative mind interwoven with life's limitations. Everyone has a slightly different look on the way things go together. So, each of us is our own work of art. And you can see it in a person's smile.

Battle of the Sexes: *Boys are better than girls. Girls are better than boys.* In our general confusion about life our gender predominates over all other aspects of our identity. Often entwined in intelligent arguments it still rarely rises above those schoolyard boasts. In reality the differences between men and women are filled with possibilities. Men and women do better working together than competing with each other. You'll find that beyond the capable person you've discovered yourself to be there's another surprisingly similar, fascinatingly different, exciting and attractive person for you to share your world with. The other sex is not the opposite sex. They're your complementary sex. They're your other half. And a sensible union can create balance and love and the power to give you everything you want in life.

Beauty & Attractiveness: Everyone forms their opinion of others from their first impression. So your personal style is an important way you communicate with strangers. Style helps people decide if they think they can identify with someone new. We're always looking for the common ground that lets us communicate with each other. We're looking for people who see life the same way we do. We anticipate being comfortable with people when their style shows we share the same interests. But beauty's uniqueness is its ability to cross the divide between styles. It inspires us with an appreciation of humanity beyond our designs. Beauty is the perception of order in the universe. Just remember, beauty's not limited to looks alone. Beauty is as much a quality of your love and dreams as it is of your appearance.

Capital Punishment: Is it right or wrong to kill someone as punishment for a crime? This is a struggle of conscience for many people. Is it against the will of God? Is it disrespectful when we believe that life is a gift from God? Is retribution justice? Is long-term imprisonment really more humane? Are executions a real deterrent so others won't commit these crimes? And is the conflict in a community's conscience satisfied by killing someone who represents a threat to it?

Human nature is to love each other but society can be pushed to its limit when it sees itself threatened. But a society using capital punishment for justice lacks the confidence to maintain its public safety any other way. On the other hand it's wise to protect yourself and eliminate the possibility of future crimes by the same person. It's a practical point of view because it's everyone's right to live in a safe environment.

So maybe to be fair we should set an age limit on the death penalty. It wouldn't allow anyone to be executed under the age of 40, for example. At 40 a person matures and starts to appreciate their life. They're old enough to understand the pain they've caused and hopefully they've learned the value of the life they're about to lose. For older criminals, a term of imprisonment prior to execution could be the sentence. This would give them time to reflect on the tragedy of their crime. Then justice could incorporate respect for God, protection for society's future, and retribution in punishment.

You have an opinion though, and ultimately it's you who decides what justice means when a person's life is repayment for a crime.

Charities: Giving to others means sharing what you have. When you share with others you're really giving something to yourself. That's the reason helping others feels good. It's satisfying to sacrifice something for someone who needs your help. The intensity of good intentions is fully embraced when you understand its opposite. It's the betrayal you feel when you realize someone's tricked you and used your donation selfishly instead of giving it to the people you wanted to help. It's worse than being robbed. It's like your love's been stolen. And the humiliation can overshadow the grace in your charity. But even when your trust fails, the love you give succeeds. God makes sure we have what we need. The only real loss is the disappointment of missing that connection of souls trying to help each other. The trust we feel in easing the suffering of other human beings is an inseparable connection. And it should be respected as the grace that supports us in return.

Children: Children are the blessings of new beginnings. The way they accept new things reveals God's abilities. Despite a baby's fragile body you can still feel their potential. And it's easy to misinterpret their small size, reliance on others, and inexperience as weaknesses but just the opposite is true. They have strength in their intensity for learning. They're only limited by what they're exposed to. They can do anything once they know how. And their love is uninhibited by the judgments we learn in society. In knowing nothing they're all inquiring. And without attachments they love everyone. They're so special because their unencumbered joy is the miracle that teaches us love.

City Living or The Country Life: We all live in a community. And it's your choice to live where you want. Every place has its own benefits and requirements. So it's up to you to decide where the demands, compromises, and return on living somewhere balance out to meet your needs.

And nothing's written in stone. If your circumstances change or you just change your mind you can always move somewhere you like better. Feeling stuck someplace can magnify frustrations and turns life's difficulties into daily drudgery. So when things aren't the way you want them, hope for a change. Don't ignore the problem. As you mature you'll understand how you judge your happiness. And you'll realize that where you live is important.

Your choice to live in a place you love will favor everything you do. A comfortable home relieves you from life's hectic pace. Your home, your neighborhood, and your town can be your refuge and the closest you'll ever get to paradise on this world. There's no right or wrong about enjoying one place over another. Your guide is in knowing what makes you happy. Your willingness to give yourself your happiness is up to you.

Community Service: Why do people help each other? Why do we volunteer our time or donate money to help people we don't even know? It's because our nature is to care for each other. In some way we all want to be friends. Then there's more to go around and problems are reduced when the burden is shared by everyone.

We give and we receive. But in truth all we ever give is love. Time and things just represent love. Sharing connects us with love in a way that we can touch it. It reminds us of the bond we have. We feel it as a debt in our souls. And we fulfill ourselves when we repay it.

Today a modest penalty for breaking the law is being sentenced to "community service." The hours involved and the service performed usually depend on the crime. "Serving time" in prison is known by a forgiving community as "paying a debt to society." But the debt we owe to humanity is a shared debt. We're owed as much as we owe but the debt is never canceled. It's a never-ending debt to the benevolence of our common nature. So it's a responsibility, not a choice.

Community service can be as simple as putting a dime in a beggar's cup but its meaning will always be the transfer of love and recognizing its unifying power.

Cosmetic Surgery: Advancements in plastic surgery have had enormous benefits for those whose lives have been changed through these procedures. Far beyond looking more attractive they hold hope for many who've suffered disfigurements. Today many heartbreaking conditions can be successfully transformed.

What once were medical marvels are common now with new techniques being developed every day. And it's important because we rely on our appearance. We communicate through our appearance. Your personality—your attitudes and emotions expressed through your body language and facial expressions—relates who you are to the world. Physical comparisons are a convenient way we evaluate each other. And though everyone's different we mostly fall into the great average. So it's the extreme cases that really benefit from plastic surgery. People who appear dramatically different stand out from the group and may miss opportunities readily available to the rest of us. People fear the unfamiliar and resist it. But plastic surgery removes those obstacles so a person can blend into the group and enjoy its benefits.

Some people elect to have cosmetic surgery to improve their appearance. They're dissatisfied with their looks and they want to look better. They may want bigger breasts, a different nose, or more hair. They may want to look younger or appear more energetic. There's nothing wrong with wanting to look your best. No one likes having a pimple let alone be unhappy about their physical features. We all comb our hair every day because we want to feel good about ourselves.

It's important to look in the mirror and be pleased with what you see. But don't torment yourself over your body. Cosmetic surgery simply moves you from one point in the great average to another. But if it's important to you, do it for yourself. It's your happiness that matters.

Death: Life has a beginning and end for each of us. We start and we finish. We take our first breath and we give our last. But life goes on and love continues in the hearts of the living. We shouldn't grieve that those who've died were denied more of life. A soul is eternal with infinite potential. People shouldn't feel sorry for themselves either. Love and its memory are great gifts and a lasting tribute to God's grace. Any opportunity to love is a blessing to enjoy. With every death though, God suffers the greatest loss. Because with every soul that passes on there's a little less love in the world.

Differences: By far there's more that makes us alike than makes us different. When you look at things together there are only fractional differences. 99% we're all the same. If beings from another planet visit us someday they'll probably be amazed that we find so many differences between ourselves. We'll all look pretty much the same to them. But we depend on these perceived differences to define our identities. And they're imagined differences because life's the same for everyone. We all have the same responsibilities. It's just the approach that's different. And everyone's approach is perfect for themselves. The rest is just details.

The criteria you use to define yourself and your picture of success aren't important. It's everyone's responsibility to choose a frame of reference they can relate to as the right way to live. Your differences are less important than what you think of yourself. Sure you can be the odd one out. You can be different in any number of ways—big, small, confident, shy, smart, dumb, or whatever. But as different as you think you are we're all part of the average.

The advantage in being like those around us is we're part of the group. Then we can take on the group's personality and have security in being personally anonymous. And we can go on about our business without having to deal with immature people who can make being different a problem for us. There's comfort in sameness because with group support you don't have to stand alone.

Sometimes you may find the wrong things to identify with about a group—its displays and ceremonies—and not its real values. And it can be disruptive instead of bringing the stability you were looking for. Real safety comes from accepting yourself and everyone else for our humanity. In every human being love opens the gate to spirit. And in spirit we all share God's love with life's possibilities.

Economic Policy: We get our sustenance from this world. The universe, our planet, and all humanity sustain us and give us an opportunity to live here. Every day these systems protect us and provide the nourishment we need to survive. Health is our physical wealth. Freedom is our emotional wealth. Love is our spiritual wealth. Curiosity is our mental wealth. And economics is the wealth of our creative survival.

Scientifically economics can be hard to understand. The important factors move to the whim of human priorities. So the factors are unreliable as a trend that can be relied on to make forecasts. And there will always be valid arguments for them meaning different things. Besides the hard economic facts of production and consumption, economic forecasts must depend on human behavior dealing with life's changing circumstances. So they can only be estimated— never predicted.

Regardless of how well you understand economics it affects you on every level of your life. Economics is your freedom. And you can learn the basics and introduce yourself to that freedom. Investment, performance, and budgeting are the same for you as they are for the biggest corporations in the world. And even if you don't have all the opportunities of some worldwide business, opportunity always exists for you to improve your economic condition and enjoy the bounty of your efforts.

Education: You can always do better. And educating yourself should be a part of your continual plan to improve your condition in the world. You'll make more money when you offer the benefits of your knowledge. And you'll get more out of the things that interest you when you know more about them.

You can educate yourself by going to school, reading, or associating with people with the same interests as you. You can go to school full-time, part-time, or any schedule that fits your lifestyle. You can go to a technical school and give yourself a career. Or you can take a course on a subject that interests you to enhance the fun you have with your hobby. Business seminars and adult education offer a wide range of topics. And there are other educational opportunities offered by mail and the Internet. You can learn computers, crafts, or current events. Whatever interests you there's someone somewhere who can teach you more about it.

Whenever you take a class, appreciate the opportunity and make the most of it. With public education the first step is to understand that it has value when you look for it. To the disinterested it's just an annoying place to pass your adolescence. But when you take a mature look, there are advantages. If you can't see them then ask someone for help. In any school there's an opportunity to gain something if you want to. You control what you do about it. So your future is up to you.

When the cost is a factor you should know there are loans and scholarships available to help you pay for it. There's always a way. You might have to make an effort to get it but the money is there for you. And you're entitled to it as much as anyone else. Society sees the importance in young people getting an education. It helps the whole community. That's the reason we have a public education system. It's to help upcoming generations educate themselves and rise to the height of their potential, because society knows their potential is the root of civilization's next great accomplishments.

Entertainment: Everyone needs recreation. We all need a break from our ambitions. We all need relief from our routines. But if you don't take care of yourself routines become your master and you can wind up a slave to their mechanical rhythms. The stress of daily living wears down a human soul. Human beings are more than mental calculations and calculated emotions. The emotional nature of our being is we're meant to be free. And while plans help us achieve our goals, life's plan never ends. Every day it asks for more. But some plans outlive their usefulness. So we need more energy to revitalize ourselves. And entertainment is the way we treat ourselves to the power in our freedom.

Whatever design your entertainment takes, it's yours. One of the ways we identify ourselves is through our pleasures. It's a big part of how we evaluate our opportunities. You know what you like when you see it on TV. You know the magazines you like to browse. And you know your daydreams. So be honest with yourself. Find out what you like. Accept it. And give it to yourself. Find a way!

We all need fun in our lives. Whether it's time with your family, physical activity, or reading, find what satisfies you beyond your survival. Entertainment is part of your learning experience. It's rest for your soul from life's dulling routines. You're entitled to it. A refreshed mind sees more possibilities. So make the most of it and have fun!

Environment: We'll either live in harmony with the environment or it won't support us. Our environment is all we have to sustain us. We can't destroy the world but we can diminish its ability to provide us with the essentials we need to survive here. The air we breathe and the water we drink give us life. And our foods depend on a healthy planet to support them so they'll always be there for us.

The balance of nature gives human beings a dependable system for living. It's a resilient balance but it has limits. Drastic changes in the environment can bring famine, disease, and suffering to humanity. And while floods, droughts, and freezes are normal for the world, they have devastating effects on living things.

We can't control the forces of nature but we can direct the power of our own nature. Our creative nature changes the world from its raw natural state to conditions that favor the way we live. But we can create changes in the environment faster than the world can absorb them. And it's possible for the balance of nature to shift beyond its ability to give us the stable sanctuary we need.

An important environmental challenge we face today is how we dispose of the by-products of our manufacturing processes. Modern society introduces massive amounts of waste into the environment. What we can't use we have to discard somewhere in spite of the problems they cause. So we have to find ways to live with our waste products as well as we live with our consumer products.

As we mold nature to fashion the mechanisms of our modern lives we affect it. We move it and we change it. And changes in the environment affect every level of human growth, from an embryo's development to the health of a body's cells in its later years. To respect ourselves and our place in nature we should respect the whole planet. We're not separate from it. We depend on it.

Fairness in Business: Industry, entrepreneurship, and consumerism meet in the marketplace. The marketplace can be the mall, a corporate boardroom, or your local grocery store. It can be a magazine catalog, your telephone, or the Internet. But no matter how you do business you should be treated fairly. We all want good value in the things we buy. If we're unhappy with the quality or price then we don't have to buy it. We do have a right though to expect a fair representation of what we're buying. You have no obligation to buy anything for any other reason than you want it. So it's in the interests of every merchant to give the best value possible—to provide good quality, good prices, and good service—so you'll come back to spend your money with them again.

But there's always competition for your money. And that means you have choices. That's a big benefit. It means there's always another merchant somewhere who'd be happy to give you what you want and create a positive business relationship with you. But sometimes it's not that easy. Some people doing business see each other as opponents—not traders. They look for pressures beyond the sale that could give them an advantage, an omission or some pretense that affects your decision. So protect yourself, be alert, and trust your common sense. Listen to what's said. Ask questions and get answers you trust. Know what you're paying for. Don't be rushed.

Don't worry that you might miss out on something. Just be clear on the terms of the trade.

Where you spend your money is your choice. And you should actively express it. You should respect yourself and expect good service. If you don't find it, do yourself a favor and take your business to someone who values you as a customer and knows how to show it.

Fashion: Fashions reflect the changes that mirror the mood of a group. It works because people enjoy collective evolution. They want to look right and fit in. But they need guidance to help them choose a direction, especially with something as imaginative as change. A change in style becomes a new adventure. So it's fun. But it has a limited lifespan and inspires only until a new look comes along.

Fashion isn't superiority or a secret badge blessing insiders. Fashion is just what's current for a group looking to define its uniqueness. It's an artistic trend to new explorations of the human experience. It runs in cycles because even with our unlimited imaginations we're still limited by nature. So we recreate things, mix them up, and push them to extremes. And the past is regularly reborn so new generations can take their turn to play with it. The details don't matter. It's only the soul's expression that's important. That's the message of fashion.

Style is in everything. It's in the way you talk, your lifestyle, and everything else you choose. It can appeal to your emotions, your physical senses, or your pure sense of being. It can be a color, a shape, or an attitude. But whatever form it takes it identifies you. We present our personalities through our style. It's an easy way to communicate with others. So we live our lives in one style or another. And we change it to suit our needs. Because it's not just our clothes that we choose with our fashions. It's how we identify with life.

Finance & Investment: How you manage your money reflects your lifestyle. Your plan could be called "aggressive" when you take greater risks but you have more opportunities for bigger gains. Or your investments might be called "conservative" where there's less risk to your principal but a lower yet more dependable rate of return. You can win or lose with either plan. What's certain is no one likes losing money. Everyone hates the limits caused by having less money to spend. On the other hand everyone's delighted in making money and celebrating the financial freedom that comes with it.

But you have options besides investing in the projected value of things. You can invest your money in yourself. You can buy an education that increases the value of what you do and the money you get for it in the marketplace. Or you could buy a new wardrobe to impress an employer. Or get a better vehicle to help your business.

However you spend your money the theme of investment is financial improvement. It means having a plan where you make more money by using the money you have. It means using your money to better yourself while you're aware that you could lose it too. A financial plan recognizes that money should be actively worked. Money represents the power of your time and effort in the same way life represents the power of God. Life demands action. And you're going to need money to activate it.

Foreign Aid: By giving foreign aid a nation helps itself by helping other countries. It's easy to see why we help countries suffering from wars and natural disasters. That's humanitarian aid. Foreign aid is different. It's the money we give other countries to improve themselves. We help them in every aspect of society—from national security to national electrification, from water management to agriculture, and from government administration to healthcare. We do it because it helps us. If it didn't, we wouldn't be so generous with our money.

What we buy is stability. We invest in other countries to create a predictable society so we can make dependable plans for our future. Foreign aid is smart because there's a limit to what one country can do to influence another. Other countries resist foreign ideas as much as we do. Worldwide immigration problems demonstrate that even the best intentions run into a clash of cultures.

Foreign aid proves that friendship connects in the souls of human beings. When neighbors prosper they feel safe. Prosperous nations are good trading partners and that means more for all of us. A nation receiving foreign aid can still express itself according to its culture. We want every nation to be free. What foreign aid does is join world security to world prosperity through the human spirit.

Gambling & Lotteries: *Get rich quick! You put down a little and get back a lot. It's the thrill of a lifetime, again and again. And it's easy. There's no waiting to see if your hard work pays off. You can have it all right now! And anyone can do it. Just buy a ticket, call your bookie, or stop by the track. And you're a winner! And hey, the lottery's only a dollar. And you can have wealth beyond your dreams, beyond your imagination, even beyond your needs. It's a vacation in Vegas or a friendly poker game. And there's no working Saturdays when you'd rather be out having fun.*

Gambling's certainly not boring. It makes life interesting, win or lose. Just follow the action. But stress can come with gambling—a whole lot of stress—because it's stressful to lose your money. Losing can be a terrible strain if you can't afford it. What if someone depends on you for the money for living expenses that you've lost gambling? Or how are you going to pay your gambling debts and your car payment too? Acrobatic desperation can overcome a person when their bills are due but their money's been lost in the excitement of gambling.

Will "Easy Street" be that secure though? Can all that money save you from life's problems? Maybe it will and maybe it won't. But however it helps you, you'll still have to get up every morning and face life's responsibilities like everyone else does.

Gambling is irresponsible, immature at best. It waits for unpredictable opportunities while planning your life creates manageable opportunities you control. Ask yourself if the excitement in gambling is real. Can you ever have real value without risking what's precious? It's not just your money. It's everything that makes you who you are—your strength, your time, your possessions, and everything else that gives your life meaning. It's when you're ready to risk everything that you accomplish what you want. That's the opportunity life gives you. That's real excitement. That's achievement. It's the big gamble and the real gift of living.

Genetic Engineering: Everyone's heard about cloning. It's duplicating a life-form by manipulating its genetic code, its formula for living. That formula includes its size, color, and just about every other characteristic it brings to life. By changing the structure of the chromosomes carrying the genes, by removing certain genes and introducing others, the idea is to influence the organism's growth and make it better. And this includes humans.

By controlling aspects of the organism's growth it's hoped to give it new directions. It's hoped to be beneficial by healing diseases transmitted through the genes or caused by genetic malformations. It's also intended to grow things that serve humanity, whether it's to increase wheat production or regrow diseased body parts.

As creation is limitless the ability to grow life to our designs has vast possibilities. But with this awesome potential, unknown risks should be considered. It's all very new. The possibilities are not fully understood and unforeseen side effects—which could seriously affect a genetically altered organism and its environment—remain to be seen.

Our human design leads us to change the world around us to make our lives better. We've redirected rivers and introduced plants and animals where we hoped to see a benefit. These efforts have had great successes as well as tragic enduring failures. So we see our best intentions can end with unexpected results. And the result of a mistake can be worse than the original problem. The effects of changing nature include growth, so they're often unpredictable. And unanticipated problems can be expensive to fix if they're fixable at all. But good or bad, we have to live with them.

It's interesting that people wonder whether a soul would inhabit a body created by science. No one knows. But spiritual life will use any opportunity where love can be created. What we create in our wisdom or shortsightedness is up to us. With love and consideration to guide us this could be another wonder we've uncovered that joins God's grace to the innate potential of the natural world.

Government Influence & Responsibility: In America we live in relative freedom secured by laws and regulations that form our social order. Our society is as intricate as a Chinese Mystery Ball whose delicately carved spheres rotate freely inside others—all carved seamlessly from a single piece of ivory. The difficulty and mastery needed to create one make me wonder how it's even possible. It's an amazing achievement. They're fascinating.

Human beings are like that. Someone will think up the strangest thing to do and with total disregard for what it takes to make it happen just go ahead and do it. It makes total sense to us to develop ourselves on this complicated world. We're complex creatures in our bodies and our minds. And we're comfortable in our universe. We live happily in the confusion because our system of laws has at its essence a desire to benefit society by accommodating its parts.

Laws vary from country to country and the standards are designed to serve the customs of that country. But people's needs are basically the same and we expect any culture's laws to be fair to its citizens. Any type of repression opposes spiritual nature. Divergent views should be respected. Laws suppressing the expression of ideas come out of selfishness, fear, and confusion. And they're unfair to a growing society that thrives on new ideas.

So how much government do we allow? How much freedom are we willing to sacrifice for its benefits? How many rules can we tolerate? It's a question of how much help we need. For whatever reason, if we need help we have to find it. And the greatest source of organized support in the world comes from a national government that can take its combined resources and focus them on a single purpose. Committed governments have rebuilt cities, cured diseases, and taken us to the moon.

Nevertheless governing is a juggling act. It must weigh the cost of a solution to the value of the need it serves. It must decide where its priorities are. How important is a particular problem? And whose problem should be fixed first? When the choice is between planting trees on Main Street and funding flood relief, common sense tells us what to do. It's deciding the things in-between that's the problem. How do we set priorities when so many people have valid needs?

And how do we insure that the solution for one doesn't intrude on someone else?

We want to take care of everyone. In the same way we want things for ourselves we want others to do well too. But there's a cost for everything and resources have their limits. So we'll forever have the challenge of choosing one thing over another and hoping that we've made the right decision. Society's complications are like a child's puzzle. It just takes time to get the pieces to fit together. But no matter how many pieces we deal with we're designed to live here. So we should be good at it.

Guilt or Innocence: What's right or wrong differs from place to place and it changes with the times. It flows to the will of a culture and the movement of its generations. It adjusts to the needs of that society. What's "right" will always be those activities considered a contribution to society. And "wrong" will be whatever's considered a threat to society. So if guilt is being responsible for doing something wrong, then it's important to be very clear on what's considered right and clearly define the limits of wrongful behavior.

The difference between right and wrong is always conditional. Each situation depends on unique circumstances to determine if an equalizing factor justifies normally unacceptable behavior. Human beings are empathetic. No one wants to be the victim of a crime but we can easily forgive someone who steals out of desperation to feed their family. We know we could forgive ourselves in a similar situation. We can understand how circumstances can force someone to do something they'd normally reject.

Whether it's a crime or necessity is something that we let government decide. We delegate the responsibility to our justice system.

There we have a compromise through an impartial arbiter whose job it is to identify what's acceptable and administer compliance.

An example of how our perception of justice floats on the moral tide is the conflict we have between the value we place on life and murder, the destruction of life. We feel sad for anyone who suffers the loss of a loved one. We cherish life and grieve its loss. But in times of war conditions change. We may find our finest citizens in situations where they must launch weapons that kill hundreds of people with the flick of a finger. And the killers are cheered as heroes with barely a thought for the victims. It's justified as necessary, an unavoidable tragedy of war. It's not important which side you're on. Any group can take this position and rationalize the rightness of murder.

But we must always ask our spiritual selves, "Was it avoidable?" "Was it the right thing to do?" "Was there any other way?" There's never a satisfactory answer when you're compelled to do something you detest. So to protect our psychic sense of social justice we must acknowledge the truth. Hopefully we find peace in our loving thoughts and consolation for our doubts in God.

The human struggle fascinates us. We're interested in anything unusual especially if it's horrible and happening to someone else. Superficially it may seem terrible to see someone's suffering as entertainment but it's never just that. We examine our own pain by comparing it to others who also suffer this life. Without that resistance there's no way to know right and wrong. So there'd be no way to succeed. And we all want to succeed.

Gun Control: Gun ownership is about self-defense. The main issue in the debate is whether a gun owner's desire for self-protection is more or less important than the danger guns represent to society in their greater availability.

When a homeowner has a gun they have the added security to meet a deadly threat. And a criminal uses a gun to terrorize their victim with the deadly force a gun stands for. But it's a false sense of security they both see in strength. It doesn't matter if it's a pistol or an aircraft carrier. They're only machines. Power is an advantage but it doesn't guarantee a result.

Just holding a gun you can feel the uncertain power of the thing. You can be fairly certain it'll fire but who gets hurt depends on human control. If you hold a gun and you think you control it you're only partly correct. The only sure thing is that it'll function impartially according to the laws of nature.

Shooting can be fun though. Sport shooting is about accuracy and self-control. It's the same as a practiced dance step or a well-placed golf shot. And it has the same satisfaction of accomplishment. The difference with guns is in the violent power they produce that causes tragic results when misused against the community.

Health: The most precious commodity you own is your health. It's your control over your body. It's your freedom to function in the world. Your health is your physical expression of free will.

We expect to be healthy. Most of us have strong bodies able to resist the strains of daily life. But everyone's body has limits. It's dramatically proved where many athletes who worked hard to improve their performance later suffered problems caused by pushing their bodies too far. Many suffer chronic pains from the extreme forces they subjected their bodies to in training and competition.

The most frustrating thing is to suffer an ailment that forces you out of your normal routine to accommodate the illness. It threatens our freedom because we have no choice but submit to it. It can't be ignored or traded away. And though an illness may not force you to give up your dreams, it can make everything harder.

It's important to respect your health. It's easily lost through neglect. Your health can be your greatest asset or the biggest obstacle to your happiness. You can't make yourself indestructible but you can show that you value yourself by doing what you need to stay healthy.

History: Everyone wants to know the future. So we read our daily horoscopes looking for the guidance that helps us predict the day's course. We want to know what lies ahead. And we want the tools that help us see it. We don't care what they are as long as they work. And simple as it seems, history is the magic window we can look through to the future.

There's enough recorded history to demonstrate a predictable pattern that can help you understand just about any possible future. Plus there's so much interest in the past that we're forever reexamining it. We've examined events from every alternative you could imagine. Today we know more about the circumstances of history than the people who actually lived them.

From the weather conditions to conflicts in politics, today we have the advantage of seeing the separate events of the past as part of an evolving mosaic of human experience. Today we can see the pattern of those forces and where their interaction led. People haven't changed. Life's demands are the same as they've always been. And human goals are the same as they'll always be. Even the variables repeat themselves. That makes everything predictable. The past, present, and future all form a single line. And like a strand of DNA, any culture can be understood from a strand of its place in time.

Your knowledge of history tempered by your understanding of human nature lays out a map of the future for you. History goes beyond repeating itself. It repeats itself regularly. History is more than the triumphs and tribulations of great civilizations. It's your daily life repeated every day in the history of humankind. History is the story of our relationship to God. And it's easily recognizable if you give yourself a chance to let history be your guide.

Humility, Embarrassment, & Humiliation: Humility acknowledges the human part of life. It sees you as an eating, breathing, consuming process of living. So humility sees you as an equal to everyone no matter what your differences are. It's not about weaknesses. It accepts your physical self as a part of you. Being humble is not deferential behavior. It's the sign of a healthy character that relies on practical truths, not someone's opinion. It's belief in the rightness of who you are regardless of your physical nature. That includes thoughtless things you've innocently said or your choice to wear some out-of-date fashion. It freely accepts who you are and loves your faults together with your love for God in everything. Beyond your emotions, intelligence, and spirit, you're a part of nature. It's the physical part of your personality.

So it's wise to love every part of yourself—warts and all. Accept everything because it blesses your ability to function as a total human being. Humility accepts all human foibles—farts, burps, hiccups, forgetting someone's name, a stain on your shirt, or going to a party with the price tag hanging off your new clothes. And it dismisses what other people think when you wear last year's shoes or drive an old car that's all you can afford.

Humility is accepting a loved one's offensive behavior when it reflects on you but is nothing like you. It's feeling comfortable when you talk about sex, compare paychecks, or go to the bathroom. And it acknowledges the guts of life without being clever about it.

We stand up to embarrassment and humiliation by accepting human nature with self-love, not self-hate. Believe it or not, humiliation is good for you. It's an opportunity to expose what makes you uncomfortable and learn to love every thought you have about yourself. And it's the same for everyone. Our human aspects don't go away just because we think they're improper.

Sometimes humiliation is used as a weapon to embarrass someone and hurt them. You've heard about people "demanding an apology"—as if sincerity could be squeezed out of someone by forcing them to apologize and punishing them with the pain of defeat. It equates being human with losing. As silly as it sounds that's what some people think. Real humility is the difference between living to please others and living for your own self-respect.

Humiliation doesn't lessen you. More so, it wants to show you another way to love yourself. It reflects the Bible sentiment that you're not better than anyone and neither is anyone better than you. Humility builds faith when you trust its guidance. It's the power in pride because pride without humility is just a boast. Humility isn't shyness or reticence. It's the self-control in self-acceptance. And it's a sanctuary for anyone with common sense. It's the comfort of being whole with your life. And because we don't always like what we do, being humble is about being able to forgive yourself too.

Being human is always perfect. You can respect others by limiting any unpleasantness someone might feel from your faux pas, but that's all you're required to do—be respectful. You don't have to be the embodiment of someone else's image of perfection. So humility can be your freedom when you love your human nature.

Humility changes everything. Ask yourself, "How does it make you feel when you think 'humility'?" You can feel your heart's tone change. You'll be either disgusted by the weakness you see in it or you'll feel comfort in its grace. With humility you accept that you're here with everyone else. And seeing fairness everywhere, it's the soul's constant generosity.

Identity: It's who you think you are. It's where you think you should be. It's how you interpret right and wrong. It's not what others think of you. It's how you describe yourself. It's the limitless consciousness and presence of mind that constantly keeps you company.

You have a pronoun identity that reinforces your conscious presence in the world. Remember, you're always an extension of God's wholeness. So when you say "you" to someone in a conversation, ask your mind if you're not really talking about yourself. It's amazing how easily your thoughts seem directed at yourself. When you talk to someone about a third person and use the pronoun "he" or "she" you may subconsciously be talking about the very person you're talking to. And they may be talking about you when they're talking about someone else the same way. Likewise, when you use the pronoun "they", talking about other people, it's a wonder how readily your thoughts apply to you and the person you're talking to.

It's because even though you see life from your own perspective, consciousness is reflective. And you see yourself in others because consciousness is unified. So the way you use pronouns is a snapshot of your psyche. It's a way to understand yourself better by seeing what your subconscious believes. And you can see how it works in others too. In your thoughts do you call yourself "I", "you", or "he or she?" "I" is your self-conscious ego. "You" is the reality of your self relating to your conscious mind. And when you use the third person "he or she", you separate from your personality and see yourself as a spectator would.

It's important because your identity is the start of every moment in your life. It's the core of your emotional self. It gives you direction. Life's resistance helps build the character of your identity. So reasons matter when you're solving problems. Reasoning is the workroom of your identity. There you have the logic of comparisons, the intuitive logic of emotions, and you have choices. And it's your choices that identify you.

Insurance: You hate it till you need it. You pay for it every day but you hope you'll never use it. So insurance is an odd thing to put a value on. It's only with a problem that it has any value and a problem is the last thing you want. When you do need it though, you're grateful to have it. Insurance can take the financial sting out of life's worst problems. So we pay to insure things against the risk that we might lose them.

The government requires at least a minimum of liability insurance to own a car. It's the law. That alone proves how dangerous it is to drive. People have a lot of accidents. Everyone knows it. So we need insurance to pay for the high cost of medical bills and property damage. And we use our cars every day. We consider driving one of life's necessities. Most people believe the freedom to drive is worth the risks. But to balance its costs we pay for insurance to have the money to pay for any damages.

When a bank lends money to someone to buy a house they require that the borrower have sufficient insurance to protect the value of the mortgaged property. They require coverage against the possibility of fire, flood, or any calamity which might reduce the value of the property. It makes sense. The property is collateral for the loan. It's the way the bank protects itself against losing the money it lends to people. In return for the loan the borrower agrees to give the property rights to the lender if they can't repay it. So to be sure the property stays in good condition and keeps its value the bank requires in the loan agreement that the property be insured for at least the value of the loan.

Just about anything can be insured. You're probably familiar with insurance covering losses from fire and theft. Your life, health, and livelihood can be insured too. Businesses have different kinds of insurance to help them recover from events which could put them out of business if they didn't have a cushion of insurance to soften the financial hardship.

Insurance is part of financial planning. It's part of ownership to protect yourself from losing the value of your assets. You do your best, but in an uncertain world there's no guarantee that you won't suffer the loss of your health or property. Insurance is part of your investment in life. It's an unwelcome expense but if you can afford it it's the right thing to do.

International Relations: We grow in consciousness of the universal nature of humanity. As human beings we inhabit this planet together. Technology's advances in communication and travel, and their generous availability, have brought us even closer together. Today we know how people all over the world live. And in the details of their lives we understand them personally. When we understand their realities we can easily know their needs. And we want to know more. Our creative nature craves the raw material in every human experience.

The world's only limited by our ability to reach out to it. Today fewer and fewer places are remote from the whole culture of humanity. Now it's possible to reach people around the world with the full potential we have as modern human beings. And it's natural for us to want to live together and benefit as a world community.

Whether we're dealing with our family, country, or planet, it's human nature to expand personality beyond individuality and relate to each other as neighbors. But in any relationship it's inevitable we'll draw personal borders where we feel most comfortable. Likewise successful international relations are a measure of cultural comfort zones. Relations prosper when consideration replaces ignorance in a balance of cultural respect. The ability for the world to live in the same peaceful environment as a loving family, with all its conflicts and personalities, is the challenge. But what's most important is to believe that it's possible.

Immigration: The benefits of immigration or the problems with immigration are related to a nation's needs. Immigration's an asset where there's lots of room and not enough people. With increased immigration there are more people to develop a society's resources. But where there's more population than resources to support them, then immigration can be a problem.

There's nothing wrong with someone moving to another country to find a better life for themselves with security and opportunity for their families. It takes courage to leave a familiar situation, no matter how hard conditions are, to take on the unknown difficulties of living in a new country and the often hazardous journey to get there. An immigrant moves to a foreign country where they can expect little support to help them get started. And besides the problems of everyday life there could be resistance from the people already competing for the resources there.

Immigration is a good solution to developing untapped resources because an immigrant will take a risk. They're willing to make a sacrifice in hope of achieving their dreams. Whatever the cost, they choose the opportunity rather than suffer the problems of the places they've left behind. They're opportunists. That's why they're so threatening to the established population. Their purposefulness is more driven and desperate because in their minds there's no place to retreat. To them it means succeed or perish. And that's a hard attitude to compete with when there's a job on the line.

Anyone who would risk their life and the lives of their family to live somewhere new and unknown to them on the chance for a better life can only be an asset. What greater resource is there than a human being? What power is greater than a human being's desire for freedom? So human beings readily push themselves towards that goal even if it means risking their lives.

People will move to where they expect a better life. So the ability of someplace to absorb more population must be managed because it can't be stopped. The natural imperative of a human soul is to be free. It won't be held back. But it can be cultivated to produce a richer, more robust society for everyone.

Laws: Laws are the rules a society accepts to respect the people who live there. Laws are the limits of communal living. This assumes the intention of government is to be equal to everyone without favoring anyone with special benefits or condemning anyone to an unfair sacrifice.

Getting two people to agree on anything can be difficult. So having millions of people in accord is a miracle of human nature. And it happens every day. Flexibility and compromise are the essence of fairness. And every situation has unique circumstances which must be considered when interpreting the law.

Life's pressures affect everyone differently. And extreme emotions can confuse the best of us. So it's a challenge to create equitable penalties for breaking the law. And the need for fairness must be balanced by penalties severe enough to motivate everyone to respect the law while staying in proportion to the damage caused by the unlawful conduct. This will always be reviewed closely because everyone wants to be treated fairly.

Communities change in the normal flow of life. And those responsible for its laws change with it. So, perspectives and interpretations of the law evolve as they accommodate the changing attitudes of a community's new consensus. And in this complex process we must each stand up for our rights to be included.

Each generation's outlook changes as it expands experience and grows in awareness. And a new generation may find benefits in changing existing laws for laws which better reflect their own attitude on the meaning of fairness. The law is a flexible condition. And it should be seen from every angle, every distance, and every just purpose to successfully serve its people.

Loneliness: The normal trial for young adults is their growing self-awareness. Refined by life's pressures they begin to see themselves as individuals in a community. And they yearn for connection with the world around them and its community of souls. We all have different tolerances for the companionship of others. Some of us need constant interaction to be comfortable. Other people's opinions are very important to the way they value themselves. And others are happier with less contact and prefer the simplicity of their own company and private thoughts. They have a solitary communion with the world and see too much contact as an intrusion. So realizing your need for contact is up to you to create.

When the measure of contact is an isolated soul it's called loneliness. And feeling alone and disconnected from love is uncomfortable. It can mean desperately missing a loved one who's gone away overnight or the distrust in meeting a stranger. But what it does is block communication because it lacks confidence in love.

Human beings are social beings and positive human contact is important to our growth. We all need someone to talk to—someone to trust, someone to love us, and someone to love. We all need help and direction. New adults need confirmation to check themselves. We need the opportunity to see how others see the world. But when we feel separate it's like we're floating away beyond help. And often all it takes to cure loneliness is a smile from a stranger or the attention of a loving pet. And though it doesn't always seem so, God's always close too.

Getting along with others isn't always natural but it's a learnable skill. It doesn't mean you'll like everyone but you can appreciate you're in the same boat. And if friendship isn't offered then you have to reach out for it. How you see friendship is a personal preference. But it's important to find friends who accept you for being yourself.

Living together means accepting different perspectives. We're all created with different paths to explore our existence. And we can choose new ones if we like. We're born with different talents too. And we can learn new ones if we want. For as many people as there are in the world, there are that many combinations of abilities that can lead to a happy life. So getting along with others needs tolerance. We need to be tolerant of the advantages others enjoy and we need to be tolerant of the burdens each of us carries.

Though you're only responsible for yourself you're never alone. It's a perception and a choice. You're always part of a community. What's important is to know when you want to be with others and when you want to be alone. It's only when you honor your feelings that you'll feel really comfortable.

Loneliness can enter our lives at any time. And it may be frustrating but it's nobody's fault. It usually comes from human weaknesses—sadness, confusion, illness, or fatigue. But whatever its cause, God's presence will always be your comforting companion.

Marriage, Divorce, & Infidelity: Human beings live together naturally in mating pairs. It's how we continue our species and increase its opportunities. Survival binds us together because we're better able to face life's challenges with help. So marriage isn't just the union of two people. It joins families, resources, and experiences. The customs may be different from place to place but the principle stays the same.

While it's natural to pair off, your future responsibilities should be carefully considered. There's an emotional intensity to marriage that goes beyond simple friendship. In a marriage the trust normally reserved for close family members is given to a stranger. And intense emotions, even when likable, can confuse our common sense. So, some people get married who'd really be better off with a different partner. It's a life-changing choice and it's usually inexperienced young people who make the decision. There's a lot at risk. And even with the help of friends and family it's still just a person's judgment.

Societies love their marriage customs and the government takes it seriously. It's a social responsibility so marriage laws must be respected. It's to protect individuals and their relations when the partners have such severe difficulties that they want to end their marriage. Divorce can be extremely stressful. A couple goes from total commitment back to being strangers but now with their lives tangled up in life's complexities. It's like separating the threads of a piece of cloth, identifying each one, and returning it to its rightful owner. Financially tied to an adversary, emotionally torn by their love for their children, and the prospect of an uncertain future can make a person feel trapped. And while the law may need justification for breaking a marriage contract, relief from suffering needs no reason. No one needs anyone's approval to be happy.

Infidelity though is about unresolved needs. People dissatisfied in their marriage may seek love and comfort outside the home. The original purpose of the marriage was to create a support structure. But sometimes the ideal of a happy marriage is lost while its needs are still there. And though the belief in the marriage is gone, a contractual obligation remains.

The plan for divorce is simple. The lawyers know all the rules. The parties to the contract must be satisfied according to society's laws. But there's a human toll too. Now what had been the center of someone's life becomes a nest of doubts. And the emotional betrayal makes it even harder.

It's different than a family member who does something bad that can later be forgiven. The forgiveness of a loving family connected by blood and tradition is more accepting than one recently built by a young couple. But that's the challenge of marriage—to build your own loving family.

Betrayal isn't unusual at the start of a marriage when a family's foundation is shallow and weak. Love and trust over time give a marriage its strength. A successful marriage grows like the proverbial tree. It matures. The marriage gets stronger as its roots grow deep into the nurturing soil of a shared experience. And like a tree it needs care to stay healthy and strong. Then it can support itself and help the whole family weather nature's changes.

Media: Your senses are your greatest physical asset. Your senses are your physical presence in the world. Sight, smell, hearing, taste, and touch are your awareness. That awareness is your guide and protection. The primal power of your senses is your physical consciousness of everything around you. That's why the media holds such an awesome potential to influence people.

The media are specifically directed at a person's senses. So it's an original influence on your thoughts and feelings. Whether it's the newspaper, TV, radio, or any thoughtfully designed mechanism that transfers ideas from one person to another, it's the same as a conversation. It "talks" to you.

From highway billboards to Internet bulletin boards, people get their knowledge wherever they can. The media may separate informational presentations from theatrical entertainment but for human beings everything's educational. And it's continual too.

It's because no one's really taught anything. We teach ourselves everything. And young people want to know what they can about this strange place where they find themselves. Life frightens and fascinates them. And music and television are the tools they use to explain it. That's why kids like cartoons so much. The responsibilities in life's clutter are filtered out making life's riddles easier to understand.

It's like that with soap operas too. Against the backdrop of these simple dramas we train our emotions to have reasonable reactions to the conflicts portrayed on the shows. And as far-fetched as the stories seem, people will use any relationship as a model to measure themselves.

Young people mimic what they see on TV to test it. So the values portrayed in the media are an important influence on the meaning of maturity to them. Maturity is the product of self-development. So it's important for society to present values to its young people that clearly demonstrate its priorities. The media's power over the senses is reactive to a child. It requires no effort on the child's part to accept it. Exposure is absorbed as the ambient background of life, like the sounds of singing birds, and not intentional messages.

The printed word is just as powerful because it requires action on the part of the reader. It requires that they focus their attention. There's an expense of effort so it reciprocally demands value. Writing zips like a laser beam deep into a person's consciousness and you can almost feel it in your body. There creativity accepts it as the raw material of experience.

You're the final arbiter though. The media are only directed at you. You process the information and make your own decisions about it. And your maturity is there to help you define the truth and give it value.

For the communicators who make the movies, play the music, and bring us the news, it's also a job. It's the way they pay their bills. So an aspect of the media is that it competes for your business. Everyone wants your attention. Everyone wants your trust. And they all want your money. Of course they want to trade good value for it. That's good business. They want you to enjoy their products and use their advertisers. A lot of talented people do their best to keep you thinking about what they're selling.

Competition in this environment leads to repetition and mediocrity. Much of the media is satisfied with meeting people's basic need for what's current instead of making the effort to elevate their message and expand human consciousness by exploring the relevance of events to the progress of people's lives. It's an odd profession that on one hand is no more exotic than selling hot dogs from a cart but at the same time uses as its product the unlimited imagination and experience in being human. The challenge facing the media is in the way it chooses to exploit this extraordinary ability to communicate with millions of people simultaneously.

Medicine: Benjamin Franklin summed it up perfectly in *Poor Richard's Almanac*. "God does the healing and the doctor gets the fee." That was 250 years ago. And it's the same today because it's universally true. Our bodies miraculously heal themselves. With medicines and procedures doctors do their best to help our bodies heal. They replace parts, remove irregularities, and kill invading organisms. It's medicine's logical remedy. Then comes the miracle prescription. Rest! Now let the body heal itself.

Incisions mend, bones knit, and infections die away. Health's restored because life does its best to survive. And doctors do their best by knowing where the body wants to go and helping it along.

The importance of being healthy can't be overstated. It's important to respect your body and protect it. Even a small malady—a pimple or a toothache—can consume your attention. A sprained ankle can make you miss work and a bad cold can take the fun from your hobbies.

Disability and discomfort from an illness demand that you acknowledge it. So your daily plans might have to be put on hold till you get your health back. We can all put up with an inconvenience to accommodate an illness but some diseases can dominate our lives. And sadly, the precious nature of good health is often realized only after it's gone.

It's important to remember that you can resist an illness. Many ailments and injuries can be avoided by being alert to your body's needs and protecting it from dangers. The human body is amazing—

both fragile and resilient. Your body wants you to survive and you can help it by considering its well-being.

Having good health insurance is secondary to staying healthy. Health insurance is something you never want to use but it's good to have if you need it. Being sick can be so frustrating that you'd pay any price to get your health back and as soon as possible too. Health insurance helps you do that. It helps you get back in the game sooner without the burden of medical bills.

Some health problems are unavoidable. But with help from friends and family we deal with them. It helps to have good advice from people who love you when you're sick. It's hard to take care of yourself when you're feeling weak, frightened, and confused. Still, good health is a personal responsibility and you can keep yours when you respect it.

Mental Illness: Who's crazy? We like to call ourselves "crazy" when we act recklessly, free from the rules of convention. But it can separate us from the common sense of our self-respect. We like to test its limits though. But it's crazy to do something someone warned you not to do. "I want to see for myself what it's like." we say. And some things are attractive even when they're obviously dangerous. If things go right, what a thrill! But if something goes wrong it could mean injury and destruction for someone. Whether it's an error in judgment or faulty equipment the result is the same—an avoidable accident happens.

Some love the opportunities life's challenges give them. They like looking over the edge to see where their curiosity leads them. If that's your pleasure, just accept that there could be problems and include it in your plans. And if you're not the adventurous type, don't let anything push you out of your comfort zone. Respect yourself and trust your feelings. They're there to help you.

Mental illness on the other hand is a disease—not a conscious choice. They're disrupted mental processes resulting in confused thoughts and feelings. And it's a simple mistake to think someone mentally ill is out of touch with all reality. While true for some, many are frustrated with being sick. And they suffer their predicament like a sore that won't heal. Just because their mental processes don't work properly doesn't mean they're unconscious to the hardships they endure. Part of them may be completely lucid while their spiritual self wanders lost in their disorganized consciousness. So they hope for help from healthy minds to make sense of their confusion. But mental illness is a lonely disease where connecting with another person can be difficult. They can feel helpless and desperate for the simplicity of an orderly mind that most of us take for granted. And regardless of their troubles their responsibilities to life are the same as anyone else's.

Like other parts of our humanity, thoughts and emotions get sick. The best chance we have to nurture a healthy mind requires a safe loving environment where a person can learn to trust themselves. We all need to learn the art of self-confident expression. And loving encouragement is the way to do it.

Mercy Killing: Is it right or wrong to kill someone to end their pain and suffering? There's a conflict between bravery and cowardice when we're forced to face life's desperate trials. People have very strong opinions on the sanctity of life versus the sanctity of personal experience. So where do we draw the line? We have the popular concept of a brave soldier fighting fiercely until there's just one bullet left in their gun and then courageously using that last bullet to commit suicide rather than risk capture and a torturous death at the hands of the enemy.

But in reality we may know someone—tragically ill or injured—who suffers terribly in every conscious moment. With compassion we want to help them. We hate that they suffer. We ask if someone trapped in that condition could have a happy life. When someone's beyond medical help and miserable with pain we question whether it's God's will that we end that person's life now or wait years for nature's course to resolve their plight. We ask, "How long is too long?" And, "Where's our place in God's plan as part of the process?" So we struggle with our love for God and our love for a loved one while we search our souls for the answer.

As public policy we've found it's safest to avoid mistakes by not allowing "mercy killing" as an option—regardless of the extent of a person's pain or the hopelessness of their condition. As a practical matter though, decisions are made daily to end this type of suffering. We call it "removing life support," "do not resuscitate," or "pulling the plug" when a body can no longer sustain itself and we end the artificial assistance keeping it alive. With an attorney's help a person can write a "living will" into their last will and testament requesting not to be kept alive artificially. Then it's clear that their wish was to go peacefully into the next life instead of existing here in some technological limbo.

Euthanasia is mercy killing. It's the ultimate way to end someone's suffering and the suffering of anyone responsible to care for them. The conflict is that we cherish life and liberty more than anything else. So the question really is, "When does physical suffering impose so much on our sense of freedom that we'd rather be dead than suffer its loss?" With mercy killing, like all things, we must guard against misjudgment and abuse. There's no second chance to reverse this ultimate decision. It's important to remember that people will firstly choose life over death. It's natural to be alive and the power in the potential of life is supremely enticing.

Patriotism: Where's the place in your busy life for your commitment to your country? Or does patriotism just mean cheering for your country in some conflict you see on TV? Is everything just an Olympic sporting event? And where's our national commitment as interdependence increases around the world?

Every culture protects its existence through self-recognition— its patriotism. Its patriotic passions are whatever that society wants them to be. Every country has its own ideals and decides its own values. Some countries are thousands of years old and have great traditions to guide them. While others, emerging from the embryonic stages of sovereignty, establish their independence from the differences that make them a nation.

Patriotism is a love for your country that goes beyond self-importance and commits your interests to the well-being of your nation. Patriotism means taking sides. It means you'll debate the issues of national interest but—despite unresolved differences—you'll meet the outside world united as a nation. And you'll stand with your neighbors to defend your common interests, protect your freedom, and support your survival. And pay whatever it costs. The true measure of patriotism isn't, "Do you love your country?" It's, "What would you risk for it?"

The critical issue with patriotism is that it has value. And in a competitive world patriotism has a price. As a nation we demand liberty and we'll fight for it. It's worth our time, our money, our comfort, and even our lives. It's because nothing has value without freedom. Today America can determine its own direction. But it's easy to fall prey to success. We've become comfortable being entertained by the drama of the price those Americans before us paid for our freedom. Beyond that we should be exploring the deeper meaning of the gift their sacrifice gives us. Because there's no guarantee that our freedom will continue.

History's strewn with the bones of great civilizations that have failed under the subtle pressure of passing time and the forgotten memory that freedom has a price. So we should constantly revive the inspiration of America's "Founding Fathers." We could celebrate America's resilience with a new holiday and dedicate a whole month to honor its story of freedom and justice.

Maybe start with a more respectful Memorial Day. Let's avoid the garish holiday sales that ignore the memory of our citizens who in solemn duty sacrificed their lives for our freedom. Let's spend that time appreciating our freedom by respecting the price they paid for us and embrace our reverence by slowing down the business of our lives like we do at Christmas and Easter.

Then we could spend the month paying tribute to what it means to be free. A month celebrating our national identity could explore every aspect of America's miraculous journey supporting freedom around the world. Every year we should take time to remind ourselves who we are as Americans joined with all people everywhere who love freedom.

We should acknowledge our heritage of challenge and achievement with self-respect and honesty. We have a lot to be proud of. Once we remember who we are we can top it off with a great Fourth of July celebration. We live in a nation of immigrants and every day we should renew our vitality with the "Spirit of '76" when those colonists became a country.

We have to remember how far we've come and realize it could all be lost. So we have to decide what the miracle of freedom means to us today. History shows that when freedom's lost it might never be regained. A month each year to appreciate America, honor ourselves, and give thanks to God is a small sacrifice, especially when that sacrifice is a gift to ourselves. And we can exemplify the unlimited love possible when a nation respects equal rights and the freedom of humanity as its national ideals.

Peace: Peace is love in action. Peace is the presence of positive relationships. Peace is the trust between people. Peace manifests the "Golden Rule." Peace respects others through self-respect. Peace means tapping into the loving spirit that flows through each of us. Peace means living your life in comfort with your humanity. And it means that your feeling of well-being with others is real. Peace isn't the absence of conflict even when it produces an environment for peace. And it's not a tranquil setting. Real peace is working together to create more love for everyone.

Politics: Politics is about policies and the power and position to enact those policies. They're the policies we accept that define our society. They're the rules and regulations we abide by. It's our social order and direction. Politics isn't about elections and personalities. And it's not a game. It's not about winning or losing. It's about the laws you want to protect you and the laws you'll have to obey.

Though it seems like a sport, politics governs our lives. Beyond the TV appearances and radio ads are the policies we live by. And the disinterested don't usually get acquainted with them until they're surprised by some law that limits their freedom.

How the government's policies affect your daily life is the real face of politics. That's why the truth is so crucial. You want to know the truth about the policies supported by a politician. Regardless what they say in their political life they'll do what they believe in. But you don't need anyone to interpret common sense for you. The facts speak for themselves. You should realize that the policy a politician promotes to their best supporters is probably what they'll do. And though "spin" is part of the process, a balanced debate can usually expose the surface of the truth.

Well-intentioned solutions for improvements in government are always wishful thinking. And every side has a way to do them from their own point of view. In the final analysis it's you who decides what's in your best interests. And you should hold your politicians accountable for what they do in your name.

Pork Barrel Legislation: We want to trust our politicians. We expect them to act in our interests. We elect them to be our voice in the forums of democracy. People in a society have representatives to promote their local position on the things that affect them.

At every level of government administration needs agreement. And agreement means compromise. Compromise requires that you clearly state your needs so they can be considered in negotiations. That's the job of our elected officials. Politicians are the action arm of the decision process. They work to make the rules that let us all live in harmony. And most important, they oversee the community's resources.

So we expect our politicians to be fair. A good politician makes the best choice for the majority with respect to the concerns of the minority. Naturally, legislation allocates money for different community purposes. It's often said in a negative way that these bills contain a lot of "pork." "Pork barrel legislation" means money is spent in a localized way to benefit just a small group of citizens. The "pork" is put into these bills by local politicians for the benefit of their constituents—the people they represent. In other words, they're doing exactly what their voters elected them to do.

So it's not a terrible thing. It's a mixed compromise where politicians must use their political wisdom to make the right decision. Their responsibility to society is simultaneous with their responsibility to those who elected them. And if they don't look out for the people they represent, who will?

Positives Attitudes: Thoughts are things. Thoughts have form and structure. Thoughts have power. And your thoughts have the power to affect *every* aspect of your life. Your thoughts can affect you in obvious ways by the choices you make. Your thoughts can also affect you in less apparent ways which may seem mysterious but are still just as real. That means you have the ability to change your thinking and change your life.

We all have real problems that create practical difficulties and suffering for us. We may lack in ability or resources. Or life's unexpected burdens may overwhelm us. Problems are an intrusion that we wish would just go away. But they're also an opportunity to be successful when we solve them. Emotional pains come when you think that your problems are irreversible and hopeless. And your thoughts become negative.

The unavoidable fact that you have to deal with your problems can confuse your thinking. And you can lose your common sense in anticipation of a problem that may not be real.

Now it's true some people can turn negative thinking into a desire to accomplish great things. They may be driven to help others or be the best at what they do—even though they're motivated by fear and not love. They can do well, but without love their achievements are limited by the negative thoughts inspiring them. When goals are guided by faith instead of reactions to negative thoughts they become super-energized by God's enthusiasm for life's possibilities.

When people have negative thoughts they can create problems for themselves. They create what they're thinking about. When someone acts out of guilt, fear, anger, or self-pity, it increases the chance of a problem. Negative feelings draw people to thoughts of failure. And they can become consumed with negative beliefs. It can affect every aspect of a person's life including their health, relationships, and ultimately their ability to succeed.

A person's life can be full of these artificial problems. The good news is anyone's life can be changed and we're all able to do it. We all have the right to choose our mental attitude. You control your destiny when you believe in yourself regardless of the circumstances. Everything has an ending. And when you have a problem it's up to you to decide when your problem should end, because you have the power to say to yourself, "From this moment on I won't allow negative thoughts in my life."

Negative thinking is a learned habit. And you can unlearn it and make it disappear. First you have to identify a negative thought as just that—a negative thought. Then think to yourself, "I will not have that thought anymore." Be patient. As you retrain your mind it'll take time for those old belief patterns to fully leave your consciousness. And despite your best efforts negative thoughts can recur. But in time they'll happen less and less until you stop having them altogether.

Then let the positive thoughts of your heart replace them. And you'll find yourself again.

Prostitution: Sexuality is part of our nature. Sex is the most physical way we can relate to someone because it's more than a physical act. It's mental, spiritual, and emotional too. Life absorbs the soul in any activity. But sexuality is more confronting than the other parts of our nature. It has the same sacred aura we reserve for talking about our health and finances. It's a matter of personal survival. So we say, "That's private!" Or, "That's personal!" Sexual relationships are precious opportunities to understand ourselves. And to understand others better too. We all mature to learn that directing our sexuality is a big part of this adventure.

Selling sex is against the law in most places. It's common though for people to willingly pay for sex. Due to this conflict, prostitution's become an icon for judgments about sex. The problem with prostitution is it's really about losing self-respect. Prostitution means a person has such low self-esteem that they'd do something against their nature to get a benefit. So it's about self-punishment as well as being a desperate way to make money. And people who make themselves victims may be drawn to prostitution's oppressive environment. Prostitution becomes a convenience where a person lets themselves be backed into a situation because they think it's all they can do.

It's up to anyone in that situation to accept responsibility and use their faith to release the power in their suppressed free will. Then they can recreate their life with themselves at the center instead of being the footstool for somebody else's world. Prostitution's not just about selling sex. It's a struggle for self-confidence. And it affects people in any job.

Punishment & Crime: How do we maintain a stable environment where we can all live together peacefully? And how do we protect ourselves from anyone who'd abuse us? What we do is create laws of conduct which everyone must obey. For those who don't obey the rules, penalties provide the motivation so they'll follow the rules in the future. Punishment and rehabilitation are secondary. What's important is creating a safe environment where everyone's free to follow their goals.

Still we should be compassionate with those who don't follow the rules. They're equal members of the human family. There are people who love them. We don't have to like them or trust them but we should love them as part of our humanity. One way or another we all have to live together. And rehabilitation has the admirable goal of helping people change their lives to accept a constructive role in society.

The problem is you really can't change anyone. We can only reason with lawbreakers and hope they'll see the advantage in being part of the community. When they can make those compromises in themselves everyone benefits. Penalties prompt people to follow the community's rules even when they don't want to be a part of it, because there's no such thing as not being part of the community.

The elegance of the legal system is that a crime is considered a crime against society. It's not a private challenge. It's the people— joined as a governing body—versus every lawbreaker. Under the law a personal offense becomes a crime against the community's effort to create a safe place for all its citizens. Punishment isn't revenge. It's justice. It's a constructive effort to maintain a free society endangered by the actions of lost souls and lawbreakers who have trouble respecting the rest of us.

Psychic Phenomena: Is there such a thing as people having a sixth sense beyond their physical senses? Probably, yes. Everyone talks about it. The new age movement, newspaper horoscopes, and military remote viewing projects are some modern expressions of these latent abilities.

Many people know from personal experience that psychic phenomena are real. But like anything else we want validation for an undefinable experience. So we ask science to demonstrate the proof so we can have confidence in the evidence. But science's inability to prove the existence of psychic powers may say more about the limits of science than it does about the nonexistence of unexplained human abilities.

Supernatural experiences are weird. So it's easy to doubt ourselves. But if you look for explanations you'll find that many people have had similar experiences. A psychic experience can be inspiring and wonderful. Or it can be shocking and frightening. It has a powerful intimacy unlike anything else in the world. But either way what you're really asking is, "How can you know more?"

Race Relations: The choice to be a good neighbor is up to you. You can choose negativity and division or achievement and mutual benefit. Race relations are about getting along with people who aren't like you. They may be different in appearance or their approach to life. But the reality is everyone's different than you. Everyone's somebody else. It's hard to notice though when everyone looks the same and is basically doing the same thing in the same way.

So race hatred becomes a convenient tool for expressing our fears and frustrations. It's a way of assigning blame to people whose only "crime" is being different and easy to spot. It takes effort to accept people different than us. We feel safe in our routines. And it's easy to be frightened by a culture we don't understand.

There's an element of truth in all stereotypes. People do have unique qualities with distinct religious, ethnic, and cultural values. But it shouldn't be a judgment against those values. It celebrates God's wonders when we share them. In a world of diverse opportunities, it's fortunate that God's given us so many paths. We're all human beings. And people of every race and culture are blessed by the love within them. That's the only quality that matters.

Recreation & Work: It's important for you to achieve your goals and have your dreams come true. It's important to have success in life. And it takes work. But you can't work all the time. So part of your plan should always include rest and play. From time to time you should refresh your energy. You'll accomplish more, enjoy it more, and do a better job when you're rested. Inspirational clarity comes when you're comfortable. Being free of distractions is an opportunity to communicate with an ever-present God who waits for your attention. And when you change your focus from what's needed to what's possible, God becomes your partner.

Recreation puts balance in your life. It doesn't mean avoiding work. Resisting work in favor of doing nothing shows a problem. Work's the way our hopes and dreams come alive. It can take you anywhere you want to go in life. From just knowing that you're using your time constructively to the satisfaction of your ultimate achievements; work is the engine of our aspirations.

Avoiding work because you're afraid or feeling sorry for yourself is a solvable problem. There's an answer to the doubts that keep you from having what you want. It's self-confidence. Believing in yourself and knowing God supports you is the easy answer. So trust your ability. It seems like a lot but it grows from that single idea. And it can culminate in one of Earth's greatest accomplishments or the simple success of a happy life.

Relationships: We live in a community but there's a special benefit in the personal relationships we have with those who share our interests. Common interests can be anything from community service to hanging out at the mall. Whatever it is, the important thing is to be clear on what you want and know what to expect. And it's important to remember that the other person in the relationship has their own expectations. So it's a good idea to have a common sense attitude about human nature and accept that under certain conditions anything can happen.

The truth is relationships change over time. They grow from hopeful beginnings but can develop into something different, good or bad. So it's smart to see a relationship for what it is, not just what you'd like it to be. Whether a relationship delivers what you're looking for or disappoints you, you should be honest with yourself. So to protect yourself you should guide your enthusiasm. You should know ahead of time how you'll handle any changes. And that can give you the confidence that saves you from having mixed emotions when a conflict occurs.

When you're clear on what you want in a relationship you're more likely to attract someone like yourself. Your intentions, in your words and actions, broadcast who you are to the world. Likewise others project their intentions. And these intentions react. They either attract or repel each other.

A lot of energy goes into romantic intentions. As in any relationship you should know what you want from the other sex. Are you looking for just sex? Or maybe you're looking for a playmate? Maybe you're looking for a trusted friend to share your thoughts and feelings? Or you could be looking for a companion to pass the time with while you look for someone better. Or are you mature enough to be looking for a partner to raise a family and build a life together?

In personal relationships you explore yourself as well as evaluate others for compatibility. After all, it's the control of your happiness you're risking. To enjoy the benefits of a relationship you're sharing the decision-making process for how you live and the compromises you'll accept. It's a big decision so it's wise to explore relationships with different personality types to see who you like the best. Simply put, the natural attraction between men and women is refined through honest self-acceptance, faith in God's plan, and the maturity to ask yourself what you really want. Then let your patience give it to you.

Religion: God's relationship to humanity is as multifaceted as humanity's relationship to life. That's the reason there are so many religions. Each connects differently with an aspect of the relationship and—from its own perspective—seeks to explain the right way to live. So with God's love any religion can be satisfying.

Every religion benefits the believer in a slightly different way providing them with supportive skills for living. Every religion has a perspective on worship—its own traditions, commitments, and values. But every religion has the same perspective that God is a higher power with a greater wisdom. Every religion believes God responds to our thoughts, acts, and prayerful ceremonies. Every religion believes that the way we honor God is in the way we respect each other with respect for God. Some religions focus on God's laws—and how to abide by them—as the way to acknowledge our responsibility. Others enjoy bliss in their connection to God and manifest this bond through the joyous celebration of their feelings. Even within religions one sect may concentrate on discipline and orthodoxy while another elevates freedom and exploration in its beliefs.

Whatever religion you decide is right for you and whichever principles you choose to live by, God will be a willing guide in your endeavor to know the meaning of your life. God's joy is to join you with love's blessing and help you explore your existence.

Sexual Choices: Choices can be confusing when it comes to sexuality. Sex dramatically involves everything about us that makes us human—our thoughts, feelings, physicality, sensuality, and spirituality. And we must interpret it all as we meet our sexuality every day in our contact with others. It involves our decisions on how we act towards others, so it's about right and wrong too.

There's a lot of advice on the importance of sexual irresponsibility and its costs—damaged emotions, unwanted pregnancies, and venereal diseases. At the same time there's no easy way to explain the right way to be sexual. The one thing for sure is we should love each other. Through today's media we have abundant exposure to sexual expression, exploration, and exploitation. "Sex sells." And advertisers use it knowing it appeals to natural instincts that can bypass our best intentions. The result is that people are confused about sex because we're constantly confronted with controlling this natural attraction.

Lacking knowledge about sex is bewildering. It's not something you learn all at once. You mature into it as a total person. But we're often afraid to admit what we don't know, unwilling to suffer the embarrassment of being ridiculed by our peers. We assume we're supposed to be experienced with sex. So we boast about it. But, it's easy to fool yourself when you believe your own bravado.

The irony is that sexual gratification is a personal passion but it needs agreement with someone else to satisfy it. So it's easy to see it as a contest instead of the enlightened experience it can be. But when you find the right person you can enjoy it as an expression of your fulfillment.

One of society's greatest achievements has been the expansion of public discussion on who we are as sexual beings. Today we question the full meaning of sexuality including homosexuality. Some people are sexually attracted to their own sex. For many it's a natural attraction. For some it's an attraction of convenience and availability as might happen in a prison or during someone's youthful quest for experience. But regardless of the situation, sexuality is a part of us and will strive to express itself however it can.

As a minority, being sexually attracted to the same sex can make self-awareness that much harder to understand. These natural human energies are foreign to a large part of society. And like anyone out of the mainstream, the confusion's compounded by a lack of information and a shortage of role models.

It's a problem for any young person to be clear on their sexual impulses. Within life's droning anarchy of opinions we want to enjoy our sexuality. We want to understand and practice being sexual. We all want to be comfortable with it. And while society can set rules of common behavior, there's no wrong way to love yourself for being who you are. So live a happy life and enjoy love with your sex.

Social Order & Manners: It's important to respect each other. And we expect to be respected. On different levels we all demand it. We all want to be sure that our needs are considered.

We show respect to be clear on where we stand in our relationships. It's important to be satisfied with our place. Showing courtesies and demanding courtesies acknowledge our self-worth in life's competitive environment. And we demonstrate the level of that respect through our manners.

Whether good manners or bad, it's the basic way we communicate what we think about others. It's the way we decide if we should stay somewhere we're welcome or find someplace else where we can be accepted. It's through our behavior—our manners and courtesies—that we show the status of our relationship. This is exemplified in the importance we put on using the words "please" and "thank you." It acknowledges someone being worthy of respect.

Greetings and salutations initiate our relations with others. They show that we acknowledge someone as a fellow human being, an equal. Formal courtesies, however casual, show respect for others. From "Hey girl!" to "Yes sir!" it's the same respectful recognition. They're just different styles appropriate to the circumstances. On the other hand ignoring someone is rude. The message of rudeness is that someone has no value. Rudeness is a lack of respect for others.

Through good manners we let each other know that we recognize their life is important to them and has meaning for us. Manners respect others as independent members of society in the same way we expect ourselves to be respected. And when we feel we're treated fairly it's much easier to work together.

Society & Class: There are always differences between people. And people feel more comfortable with others like themselves. We like being with people who share our background. There's comfort in familiarity. So we stay together to support our common interests. It's human nature. But definition as a distinct group may include exclusive privileges. And not sharing opportunities is unfair to outsiders.

That's the problem with dividing people into classes. It's an easy rationalization to justify unfairness.

Everyone experiences favoritism. People at work treat us differently than how our family treats us at home. And we'd do more for a friend than we'd do for a stranger. So we look for our place in life's hierarchies and define others by their place too. A hierarchy is the relative position of those in a group and their priority in receiving its benefits. So we want to know where we are in relation to others. It's the place where our ambitions begin.

Hierarchies develop in business, family, or any group where the members' contributions vary. We honor those who make the biggest contribution. And we expect deference from those who contribute less. You can visualize it as a corporation where there's a president, vice-presidents, supervisors, and workers. Each is responsible to those above them and responsible for those below them.

Likewise social order divides by the qualities each group contributes. The placement of each class is determined by its perceived value. These groups often separate by economic status or special abilities like religious leaders, warriors, or workers. You know about cliques at school where groups of friends are attracted to each other for whatever reason. The mistake is to think that belonging to a specific group makes someone better than anyone else, because personal superiority doesn't exist in the balance of eternity.

People divide themselves into classes. By the circumstances of our birth we're inclined to one path or another. But the beginning is just a part of our destiny. So it shouldn't be used as the sole judgment about a person. Seeing people as one class or another is just one way we try to make sense of our diversity.

Society is always working to make its creativity more efficient. The value it attaches to anyone's importance changes with its needs and the qualities it perceives as most important at the time. In reality the biggest contribution anyone can give is their love. There we're all equal.

Sports: Are you good at sports? Does it even matter? Who do you have to impress with your mastery of basketball? Or who do you want to marvel at your skill on a skateboard? And what exactly are you trying to prove? You're already greater than anything you could imagine. But we're still fascinated by our ability to challenge the world just for the fun of it.

Sports and games are wonderful creations for exploring life. Our bodies are the physical extensions of our spiritual selves. Our bodies are our contact point with life. And sports are part of this exciting relationship we have with our physical consciousness.

Sports are a pleasure because they challenge us in a safe way. While competition is our way of life, sports turn life's limits into fun. It's not about work or survival. It's about exploring your living spirit. Participating in sports is like singing. First it's about enjoying yourself.

Comparing your skill at sports to somebody else's doesn't measure your success. Everyone's ability is a little different. And each person's experience contains the unique opportunities they need to succeed. Success at sports comes when you're active in them. And you participate in your happiness.

As children we loved inventing games to play. And as adults we're still looking for ways to materialize that free expression we feel in our bodies. So we like pushing the boundaries to amaze ourselves what we can do. Alone or on a team, with animals or machines, sports are the pure joy of being alive in your body.

Suicide: Life can be hard sometimes. And your happiness may seem hopeless. You might believe you'll never get a chance to have what you want. Problems may wear you down and push you beyond your endurance. Your enthusiasm for life—the power in your beliefs—may desert you. And you can lose your motivation to go beyond your problems.

Some people suffer their whole lives chasing lost dreams. And a person's best efforts can be defeated. Love can be lost and our greatest joys crushed into nothingness. And relief from disappointment may seem impossible. But your life is your creation. And your spirit helps you along the way. It can't be overcome by anything. Accepting defeat is a choice. After a misery, accepting reality decides how you feel about a problem. Things change but happiness is your goal, not any particular situation. Even when the pain seems unbearable, your soul tirelessly pursues its satisfaction. And you'll never have to deal with more than you can handle. So there's never a reason to give up. You can only be distracted by a problem and then make it more important than it is.

The problem is someone in an extremely depressed emotional state may reach out for anything with the appearance of relief—including killing themselves. So it happens when a person's in the worst shape to make a decision.

The best path for anyone in severe emotional distress is to immediately seek help from their friends, family, or community. People need help to be directed out of their cycle of painful thoughts. When you're feeling bad and you can't think straight you have to find someone you can trust until you regain emotional stability.

When you're feeling lost or lonely it's important to stay in touch with the world. You're not alone even if it's a stranger who helps you.

That's where friends come from. And friends bring you back to the reality that love surrounds you. Problems often seem less ominous after a shower and a good night's sleep. Then you can use revitalized energies to sort out your problems instead of dealing with them when you're exhausted. Remember, there's nothing new in the world. Whatever problem you have, there are others who've been through it and survived.

Survival doesn't mean your problems disappear. It means that your attitude is empowered towards your problems. It means you're willing to accept the responsibility to deal with your problems. Your confidence will come back. And your problem—instead of the focus of your life—can return to its place as a passing condition.

Our problems and achievements are footnotes to the whole person we are in a lifetime. And whatever you think you're missing, appreciating what you have is the gratitude God values. Problems pass away as time matures us. And with maturity we let ourselves move on and enjoy life even when it's different than what we first expected. You can live through the worst problems and still find accomplishment in life. Waiting is hard medicine to take when you're hurting, but patience is the cure for all emotional pains.

Patience and hope—believing in time that you'll get what you want—are the elements of faith. And your trust gives God an opportunity to return your love, encourage your beliefs, and bring you back to your wholeness—a creative human being with all the possibilities of life.

Technology: Technology is the design, manufacture, and implementation of any device that makes effort easier. It can be as simple as a nail or as complex as a nuclear reactor. It's not separate from us. It's our extension into the universe. It's never beyond us. It finds new ways to satisfy our yearning for what life offers. Technology is our ride through this wonderland. It just needs our imagination to lead it.

Imagination serves creativity. And creativity serves God's expression. God expresses on Earth through humanity. And humanity thrives through technology.

Anyone can understand why we need technology. When we want something beyond our reach we need a way to get it. And when we reduce our limitations we have more power to explore life. Then we can achieve more with less effort. Technology makes us stronger and faster. It gives us more control. We can go farther, lift more, and last longer—all with the help of technology.

The problems with technology have nothing to do with technology itself. Technology's neither good nor bad. It's only available or it isn't. The confusion comes from deciding if we really want the changes technology brings, and if we're willing to pay for it. And the confusion grows because there are always promoters for new technologies even when we aren't convinced that we need them.

Even with an easier way we might still like the old way of doing things. Some work is satisfying. We like the feeling of control that comes from physical work. We enjoy making things with our hands. We take pride in our craftsmanship. When something's handmade it usually means that more care's been put into it. Besides, we're happy with some technologies just the way they are. Some things are designed so well that a change isn't needed.

Change isn't always progress. The biggest problem with technology is becoming dependent on it. We start judging ourselves by our technology instead of valuing ourselves by the love in our lives. Instead of gratitude we begin to identify with the marvels and take their potential for granted. The truth is once our needs are met technology just has us moving faster with a bigger burden of information. We need to remember technology's a path—not a goal. Life is the goal. And there's no schedule for making the most of it.

There are many conflicting values that are equally important. Technology's usefulness is one of them. Technology affects everyone differently. So we must decide for ourselves its meaning and value. Cultural shifts in technology may not interest everyone but they inevitably affect us all.

Traditions: Traditions are links in the chain of time that join generations together. Traditions can be the wisdom of lessons learned or a maze of ancient fears. Traditions can illuminate a culture's identity or trap that society in the outmoded rhythms of its past mistakes. Traditions are the gift of experience but we must judge their value in contemporary terms.

A society's understanding must grow or its old ideas confine it. When our bodies grow we need new clothes to fit us properly. Likewise our perception of ourselves grows. And like a pair of pants grown too tight, old expectations are uncomfortable if they don't fit reality. Traditions are treasures that give us a sense of belonging so we can focus on our daily challenges. Life is overcoming challenges. And traditions provide the foundation to meet them.

Many traditions glorify our identities. They celebrate the pride we have in who we are. They show the beauty in our diversity. They remind us where we came from and encourage us to do well wherever we go. The unifying power of traditions is only limited by the respect we give them.

Traditions are opportunities to reinforce the foundation of society beyond the present, back to the past, and on into the future. Today it's our honor to protect the traditions carried on by past generations so they can serve the generations that follow. And it's our responsibility to remove negative traditions, renew vital traditions, and create fresh traditions that together form a reliable base for a new generation to build its future.

Unions: Unions are created when people realize that they're more powerful with a partner than when they meet their problems alone. People see they can achieve more by cooperating with others than just by depending on themselves. Unions mimic our natural desire to help each other. They're life's common sense approach to getting things done. Unions combine our strengths to create a force greater than what just one person could achieve.

A union can be any kind of partnership. It can be a marriage, a labor movement, or a government. The unions of men and women create the potential for our species. Labor unions provide employee organization for negotiations with businesses. And unions of governments combine cultural strengths to bring security and prosperity to their citizens.

Unions are an effort towards goals. They represent purpose in a common voice. Unions appreciate the power in cooperation. They sacrifice some individuality but in return increase an individual's ability to have what they want. And while someone's character might weaken under life's pressures, the strength of a union supports the character of its beliefs. Whatever difficulties there are in forming a union, the power of its membership working towards a common goal creates the strength needed to defend its interests and accomplish its purpose.

Victimless Crimes: Everything we do affects those around us whether we mean to or not. So we have an irrevocable responsibility to each other. Love connects us but there can be a conflict between our right to live how we want and what our neighbors want. Life's challenge is to harmonize these differences. Most of the time we get along but sometimes someone's lifestyle interferes with their neighbors. And it doesn't have to be intentional.

It can range from an irritating nuisance to being a real danger. But inconsiderate behavior is an imposition on the community. Drugs, alcohol, prostitution, gambling, risk-taking, bad hygiene, or any other activity with a self-destructive aspect can potentially move the burden of a person's responsibility from that individual onto society. When society is forced to accept responsibility for the sake of the community it becomes a victim. So in fairness we must ask, "Where do we draw the line that protects someone's rights so they're in balance with everyone else's?" And to be totally fair we must recognize that our first responsibility is to the community that supports us all.

Violence: Physical or emotional violence is the most intense reaction to a conflict. We usually see it causing an injury because whatever form it takes it's always destructive.

For most, it's the last situation we'd want to encounter. We avoid it if we can because we all want to feel good. Life's hard enough without worrying about someone trying to intimidate you with violence. That would force you into the ultimate unfairness—having to choose to avoid an intentional hardship rather than do a fair trade. That's the difference between a partner and a bully. And sometimes it's the hard choice between freedom and slavery.

Freedom as a principle of civilization is why most societies reject violence. We abhor the inequality convenient to violence. So instead we choose a system of courts to resolve our differences. Justice must deal with violence. Wherever we find it, from any point of view, we must understand it and either justify or condemn it.

We experience violence when we act hostile towards someone or when they act hostile towards us. It's dangerous and we fear it. But when we're safe from it, it's fascinating. And we want to know more about it. Like a flood or a hurricane, we want to know we can survive it.

Violence isn't a plan. It's a reaction. It goes against the prime social tenet to work together to form a cohesive society. We want friendship but we're forced to survive in competition. But violence represents the breakdown of cooperation in communicating our differences. It claims there can only be one winner. And while there may be a perception of someone winning, violence makes us all losers. You can defeat someone but winning doesn't start till there's a constructive benefit.

Even the great fights for freedom have had a downside. There's no joy in violence as a means of survival. It's the expensive road taken because there's no other choice. And at some time in the future, once the threat has passed, remorse returns as a sane society seeks to reclaim the positive history of its nation's soul.

When someone values hatred they may feel safe in their defenses but they suffer the pain of their own hard feelings. Revenge doesn't answer hate. It's just limited relief for what are really communication problems. Justice, clarity, action, and persistence solve problems, not self-indulgent emotions—especially not one as self-destructive as hatred.

So it's important to respect your enemies as human beings. Though you may never agree, you can appreciate the dramatic differences God's created in the world. And with respect to conflict, we must accept justice before degenerating into violence.

Wealth: Wealth is about comfort and security. It's feeling safe enough to expect life to be reasonably challenging without the constant burden of survival. Wealth is a state of mind where you're free to be yourself.

Everyone wants enough and no one likes the instability in trying to anticipate an unpredictable future. No one wants to deny themselves anything either. So wealth is about abundance in a situation that constantly seeks renewal. That situation is life.

The most important thing to understand about wealth is first you have to know what you want. In the safety of your private thoughts, what about life attracts you? And how much of that is just the effect of good advertising? How many of your desires are because everyone else is doing it? And how many of your desires are real from your heart? Real wealth is having your heart's desires. And it's the comfort in being able to create them.

In a demanding world wealth can mean unlimited diversions for avoiding life's pressures. But besides the material things, wealth gives a person the power to create something bigger than they ever could have done without those assets. Wealth can be money, fortitude, or friends. Wealth is anything that can be increased to help you have a happy life.

There's a difference between wealth and riches. Wealth is having as much as you need, no matter how great your needs may be. Riches are the difference between what you need and what you have that's more than what you need. Some people really need houses in different cities, jet planes, and hundreds of millions of dollars to support their needs. Wealth isn't a judgment. It's knowing what you want and being satisfied having it. So someone of modest means can have a priceless treasure because some things can only be valued in human emotions.

Wealth isn't about spending as much as you can. It's about being comfortable using what you have to enjoy the life you want. Once your needs are met, the best use for riches is to create more love in the world. And you'll decide how you share them. The pleasure you get in giving is your love returned to you. And that's having the best of everything.

Confusion over wealth comes when we feel poor—the opposite of wealth. It's when we feel unable to negotiate life. And life's a constant negotiation. So wealth is a trade-off, a compromise with what's important at the time.

Sure, you can work hard and still be ineffective at obtaining wealth. Being ineffective is frustrating and poor performance is embarrassing in a social world. And the world can make you feel like an outcast. Society looks down on those without money because it reflects failing at survival—everyone's primary drive. People want to be around success while they work at achieving their own. And they'll avoid anything unsuccessful in fear of their own failure.

Despite how we're perceived, our success depends on us believing in ourselves. God's blessed us with ability but it's up to us to use it. What you do with this gift is your responsibility. The value you create in yourself is your investment in life. In return, life will give you anything you want. Who you are and who you become is your wealth. Where you see yourself and the path you take is your wealth. But how you share your love with others is your true wealth.

Success is your right. It doesn't depend on anyone's opinion. Real wealth is your love, intelligence, and creativity. That doesn't mean you have to be smart. All it takes is a good idea and your desire to make it happen. With God, that's all you need to solve this riddle.

Weight Control: Being happy includes being happy with your body. It's the uncompromised satisfaction you have with everything about you. So dieting is about being comfortable. It's being comfortable in your clothes. It's being comfortable with your stamina and agility. And it's feeling comfortable that you can control your body. Society measures people by their appearance because it's usually the only information they have about you. But being comfortable with the positive image you have of yourself is what's really important.

Repressed feelings may be accommodated by the way we treat our bodies. We may eat too much or too little because it nurtures our beliefs. So a person's physical appearance can be a good reflection of their emotional constitution. The difference between what a person believes and their normal balance is their self-confidence in expressing the honest feelings that make them who they are. A person's body reflects good health when they accept themselves.

Weight control is about your ability to control what you eat. It's control of your appetite and the choice of foods you eat. It's the strength of your will over the power of your mind and body. Your appetite is a natural force of survival so controlling it to adjust your weight can be hard. But when you commit to a diet you enjoy the power of your self-control together with the achievement of having a body you like.

Respect for our diet raises our natural drive to survive to the heightened wisdom of good health. Gaining weight or losing weight might not be important to you. It's your comfort that's important, not your pants' size. But your body connects you to life so it's meaningful to your identity. To other people your body may be nothing more than social gossip. But to you your body is your comfort. And it's what you're willing to do about it.

Welfare: Having a good life is everyone's dream. And when we're happy it's easy to wish the same for our neighbors. But for whatever reason some people are less fortunate than others. It could be the result of an illness or bad judgment. Misfortune can start in the tribulations of childhood or a failed upbringing that blinds them to what they can do. But no matter how it happens, some people can't sustain their lives by themselves. And because we're one in spirit we don't like them to suffer.

But life is hard work for everyone. So how much harder is it when we have to support someone who should be supporting themselves? But what is the cost when we shirk our responsibility and leave the unfortunate to fail? Better yet is our glory when we bring those in need back into a constructive society.

Whether it's a village or a city, the plight of the poor affects the whole community. Like a wheel, the community's strength is in its integrity. Though parts of it can be in great shape, it still can't be its best without a minimum standard being maintained at every point on the wheel. And we serve ourselves when we know it.

The real question is, "How do we give to others so it helps them become contributing members to society?" Or, "How do we receive assistance and use it to help ourselves join the functional parts of society?" We should all be ready to research, debate, and experiment with ways to solve this problem fairly. Both givers and receivers have a responsibility in finding an effective means to social success. We all want a plan that works.

What's important is accomplishing the goal of welfare—a successful society responsible to its citizens. Changing conditions require that special consideration be given to different segments of society at different times. Natural disasters, economic turmoil, and human challenges all demand attention. Problems occur when inattention, irresponsibility, or institutionalization deaden our consciousness to the objective of society—working together for our common good. Practical ambitions and sincere efforts inevitably succeed. Work is the solution to welfare. And there's always something we can do to move forward.

Youth's Dilemma: Being young is learning how to integrate your growing self-reliance with the challenging world around you. The unique problem facing today's youth is the scope of the ideas entering modern conscious thought. In today's communication frenzy we're rapidly exposed to information from all around the world. It's hard enough for anyone to absorb it all let alone relate it to their life. This is the challenge of the "information age." And it's the next logical step in human evolution.

Progress is the goal of the special consciousness human beings were designed for. But too many ideas can overwhelm a young mind. It's like going to a restaurant with a hundred page menu. There's too much information and not enough guidance. And you have to decide what to trust in the short time life sometimes gives you to make up your mind.

We automatically process the information our senses gather and absorb it as useful potential. But too many ideas can bury common sense in white noise confusion. Being so much, instead of sorting it out you might ignore it, shut it off completely, and wipe it all away in a single stroke. And that could lead you to seek advice on things you're better off handling yourself.

Contributing to this onslaught is the fact that technology's brought entertainment and communication to the point of constant portability. Cell phones and music players are a common sight. And with laptop computers we can take the Internet with us wherever we go. But you can overindulge your distractions. And you risk missing the challenge in life's uncertainty. Because it's in unpredictability that life gives you its glories.

When things come too easy you may not realize how important they are. Today's pace is so fast that it often takes a disaster to bring us back to appreciate what we have. Many things are more valuable in the effort you make to get them than in actually having them. Your personal accomplishment builds confidence. Convenience just gives you more time. But it does create opportunities. Your nemesis though is ease because your ambitions feed on your efforts.

So you risk the real taste in your accomplishments. Technology can breed self-importance when your creativity is fooled by what you think is the invincibility of machines. We have an important relationship with technology. But we must guard against identifying with its power and beauty instead of exploiting our ability to use it.

It's important to feel your own power. Our emotions guide us around life's obstacles and direct us to its blessings. They give us the balance we need to prosper. So they give our lives meaning. Your meaning comes from knowing yourself and realizing the opportunities you have. The principles you live by are your responsibility. And like everything else in life, it takes a short time to learn the basics but a lifetime to learn their value. You can go beyond today's synthetic creativity and return to your rightful place as creator of your dreams. You don't have to be an observer tricked by the image of activity. You're alive and you can live your life's reality. It's only up to you to turn your identity into a reality you love.

Youthful Offenders: When you're a child not too much is expected of you. Not too much is expected of the problems you cause and not too much is expected of your judgment. Childhood's the time for education. It's when we're taught the basics of how to live. In play we teach ourselves through our discoveries. But we question adults to explain them. The time for our adult responsibility comes when we find that we can trust our own judgment.

Most parents raise their kids hoping they'll grow up to be successful adults. But we all grow up as individuals. And as you mature you see that you affect your circumstances by your choices. You feel the power in your presence and the strength in your awareness. At the same time, youth's outlook can be short, narrow, and shallow. They have a limited view of what happens when things go wrong or how to exploit a benefit. And it takes years to learn that we live forever with our past behavior.

In young adulthood you feel your self-control and you want to engage life. You want to see everything that's new to you. You want to do the exciting things you find. And you want to master it all. We all want to believe we can make life give us what we want. And we want to be confident about it. But confidence needs proof. Young people crave the power in that knowledge like it was the air they breathed. It's the proof they can survive here. But it needs accomplishments to make it real.

But for many the resources aren't there. That includes money and opportunities. But most of all it's the loving guidance of a caring adult that's missing. What's common to each generation is the expectation of a challenging life. That never changes. At one time there were oceans of water to cross. But today's young people must cross the ocean of information we've created. It's not a bad thing. Growing societies naturally create new problems. And it's a new unknown for everyone. But that doesn't make it any easier. Only society's best intentions and youth's innate abilities make the crossover possible. And like the New World, its potential awaits us.

Crimes committed by young people are about the careless use of their increased abilities. A young person's insatiable desire for experience can be uncontrollable. So it's up to mature adults to show them how. But young people may make mistakes that affect their neighbors. And when someone suffers unfairly there should be justice. So, youth's inexperience can have a high price because youth is a reason, not an excuse.

Guidance has meaning. And a new adult should seek guidance before they have to meet their problems in the court system. Punishing youthful offenders stains everyone involved. It doesn't relieve pain, protect society, or advance good behavior. If young people are without guidance then society must fill that role. Young people need wholehearted loving guidance to know that they're a part of life. And it invokes God's wisdom to balance justice with the morality in being young.

Zoning: Zoning is the civil expression of consideration for others. Zoning organizes a community into areas that allow everyone to do what they want while limiting the intrusion their activities have on others. It separates the peacefulness of residential areas from the hustle and bustle of business areas. Zoning separates garbage dumps with their noise and odors from entertainment areas requiring an appealing ambience. And it creates a place for schools and parks safely away from highways and industry.

Human endeavors have different needs. And their elements must work together to serve everyone. Zoning is the thoughtful design of time, space, and activity to create a total environment where people can live together without interference. Zoning is a compromise for everyone's convenience.

There are bound to be conflicts where there's growth and divergent interests. Zoning is the fairness in town planning that balances those interests. So zoning regulations must accommodate a locality's future. It serves the whole history of a community. It can preserve an environment by restricting development or enhance the local economy by favoring growth. Regardless of the direction, zoning is a community's most important tool for keeping itself vital.

WHAT'S IT ALL MEAN?

So now what do you think? Remember, it's important to see an issue through the responsibilities of those affected. It's important to be conscious of the facts, honor what's fair, and recognize that things in life evolve. That includes your opinion. So keep your thoughts fresh and your feelings open as you learn more about things—and more about yourself. You can always change your mind.

The next time you want to examine something, why not try this?

Step #1: Start by looking at your feelings. What's your first impression? It says something essential about yourself and where you stand instinctively on an issue.

Step #2: Look at all the arguments—both for and against it. Take both sides. Defend both sides. Then challenge both sides. Pull them apart, look inside, and see where they came from.

Step #3: Look at the character of the people making the arguments. Are they telling the truth? Or do they think it's the truth because they believe it? Look at their priorities. Look at their history.

What do they value? What do they think is fair? What motivates them? What do they want? Do you think they're right? Do you think they're sincere?

Step #4: Look at the facts. Do the facts make sense? Do you have all the facts? Are the facts accurate? Are the facts being interpreted correctly? Are the facts important to the issue?

Step #5: Look at as much of it as you can. Research it! Question it! Question yourself about it! Find out what you don't know. See how others look at it and what they don't know. Then question the answers. Identify the elements. Learn how the issue functions, how it acts, and reacts. What's it supposed to do? And why does it do that?

Step #6: See who benefits and who pays for it. Are the costs and benefits shared equally? Is anyone being treated unfairly? Are any costs being disguised? Are there any hidden rewards? Are the facts being manipulated to favor one side over the other?

Step #7: Look at where it came from and where it's going. Where was it born? How does it grow? Where will it go from here? What affects it? What's its effect? Who does it affect? What if it didn't exist? What if it was everywhere?

Step #8: Look at yourself. Do something. Be honest with yourself, use your common sense, and make a decision. Life requires thinking. Life requires feeling. Life requires choosing. And you'll make the right choice because the soul of logic supports your sincerity.

Deliberating is a compromise. So you have to be able to see situations from other points of view. At the same time you have to keep your own perspective. And you should always be ready to compare the facts and reexamine your opinion. We assign values. And we accept differences. And an agreement must respect all points of view to be acceptable. Compromise eliminates the undesirability in a situation while providing the greatest opportunity for everyone to get what they want.

Agreements need creativity to find alternatives people can live with. Conflicting beliefs can't be argued so they must have a way to live together in harmony. The answer to controversy is in cooperation. It understands that all goals are a complement of smaller goals that are less important than what's really wanted. And it's having a fair approach to people's concerns and the commitment to caring about them.

SPIRITING AROUND EXERCISE

Look at any issue. Then go through it using the eight-step process. It'll help you to make your conclusions. Then decide for yourself what you will.

Think About It — Chapter 5

Thought #1: *A wide range of issues affects you personally. Or they affect you as a member of society wrestling to decide what its values should be.*

Thought #2: *In a free society we try to draw reasonable borders that respect everyone.*

Thought #3: *When boundaries are crossed or thought to be crossed, conflicts can occur.*

Thought #4: *Everyone's opinion has a purpose worthy of respect.*

Thought #5: *You shouldn't take sides till you consider an issue.*

Thought #6: *It takes courage to defend the truth you believe in.*

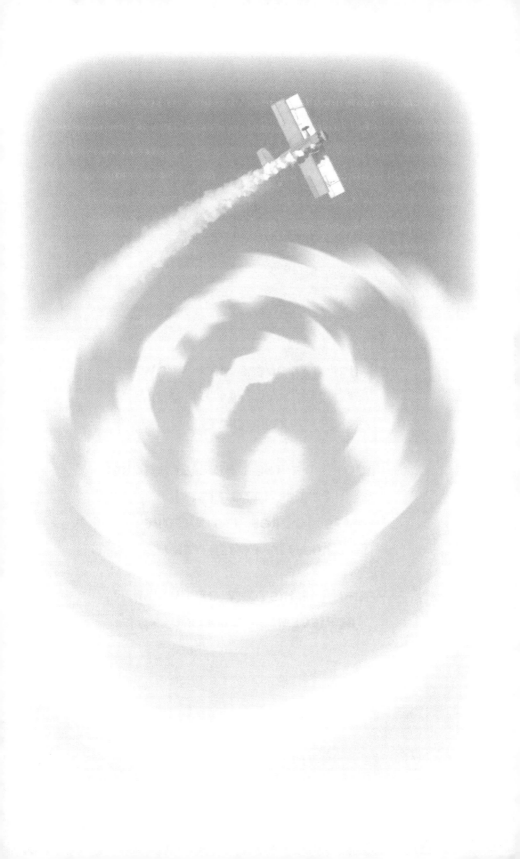

CHANGE UNCOVERS NEW ANSWERS
TO THE MYSTERY OF OUR
EXPERIENCE.

THROUGH US THE UNIVERSE LOOKS
DEEPER INTO ITSELF
—ITS SOURCE, ITS NATURE,
AND ITS POTENTIAL.

AND THE HISTORY OF HUMAN
ACHIEVEMENT CONTINUES.

CHAPTER 6

THe EXpedition CONtiNUes

Each of us is an adventurer, a searcher looking for the meaning of our dreams. We share a common nature. And we have the same gift of consciousness from God. So we face the same fate of aligning our lives to God's purpose. Life's process is a continuous experience. Intense, mild, direct, obscure, rare, or common; our day-to-day experiences can be so absorbing that it's easy to lose a sense of ourselves. But when you demand value from your experiences, everything's worthwhile. That doesn't say you should be happy with your problems. But there's value in everything and you're entitled to life's benefits however you find them. So don't waste a problem. Though you may feel the price is too high, you can find satisfaction in knowing that it's worth it.

INDiViDUᴀLiTy MEᴀNS YOU' HᴀVE ᴀ CHOiCE.

From our first breath the search for meaning begins and it goes on until our last breath signals our completion here. In that time everything's a question. Every situation's a mystery we're meant to solve. So we're always asking ourselves, "Where am I?", "What's happening?", "What do I want here?", and "What should I do?" Those are the essentials of being alive—self-examination and the constant search for answers.

From our daily chores to our dreams for the future we're always thinking about something. It's because each of us is a miracle of God's evolution. As kids we delighted in the adventure and shouted, "Watch me! Look what I can do!" Then as we grew socially we matured but withdrew into, "What will they think of me? Will I be safe the way I am?" So we seek security in groups and cling to acceptable ideas.

But fashionable ideas are not real expression. Mostly they follow someone else's expression. They're a prescribed set of choices that fit an image. And they interpret life in a way that resonates to others of the same image. So they make the adventure easier to handle. A person can feel part of the group instead of feeling their uniqueness in conflict with the world around them. As that it's fine. But fashion is the antithesis of self-exploration when it puts walls around its rules—because walls can separate you from who you really are.

When we don't know what to do, rules give us control over our lives. Even fashionable extremes must follow rules, and fashion's harsh enforcement is to ridicule what's different. It believes that being ridiculed is the ultimate disgrace. It believes that being out of fashion means to be an outsider and wrong about what matters in life. It means someone might discover the truth that you're human and not the superhero you think you have to be. Fashionable ideas are about being accepted by a group when you can't find anything better somewhere else.

In contrast, exploration reaches out from that safe place on life's carousel to risk losing your balance when you grab for the gold ring that represents who you really are. It's the search for personal identity by people who know that they're trying to find themselves. That means clarifying your identity, separating from the pack, and accepting yourself for who you are. That's maturity. And enjoying the help of the group while you work things out is perfectly okay. Fashionable ideas are a safe place to develop your confidence until you trust God as the true sanctuary of your consciousness.

ADVENTUROUS IDEAS

Extreme ideas can be expected because they're an important part of a growing personality. Testing extremes is the meaning of exploration. Society evolves by reaching for new things. And consciousness is the engine of that evolution. But when extreme ideas are divisive, exploration stalls. Then a society may feed on itself instead of exploring the possibilities God's given us. God's love is humanity's willing partner and the natural source of its creative strength. So we ask God for direction. But without the spirit of adventure direction can become a stagnant pool of self-judgments. And those judgments' rigid rules may force us into a harsh sense of ourselves.

ABSOLUTELY PERFECT

You can ridicule the most insignificant detail about someone just because it makes you feel good that you're not the one being ridiculed. You might think you're safe because someone else is wrong.

But justification's never needed to see anyone as anything but perfect. And life's meaningless details are the least of it. We cling to these beliefs because we lack confidence in any other protection for ourselves. We guide ourselves by differences to steer clear of the confusion we have about the choices we have to make. Looking to blame someone for human nature we usually pick the most vulnerable targets. Sadly then we miss out on their adventures. And when we reject our differences and replace them with self-indulgent criticisms we're really rejecting God.

The thoughts we have about ourselves are the same thoughts others have about themselves. And the thoughts we have about them are the same thoughts they have about us. When we feel confident in ourselves it's easier to trust someone else. But where there's distrust we defend ourselves. So, withdrawn behind defenses, exploration ceases. Exploration only thrives when we trust each other and praise everyone's adventure as worthy of Creation.

WHy EXPLORE ANyTHiNG?

Why bother? Why not just let things happen and enjoy what you can when you bump into it? Go for the pleasure in life. Feel good! Go for the fun! Why struggle with anything? Because resistance creates opportunities and God loves opportunities. We may dismay in the frustrations at the heart of this adventure but we benefit when we see them as chances to understand ourselves. You always matter. The purpose of any situation is to serve you. And God's concerns reach from your forgotten memories out to the edge of the universe. There's nothing too small for God's attention or too great for God's commitment.

Changes uncover new answers to the mystery of our experience. They reveal new questions as we look at what's exposed

ART OR SCIENCE?

Art and science ask questions. "Where did it come from?" "Where's it going?" "What response do I expect?" "What if I change it?" Art and science explore life differently but they're aspects of the same journey. And they nourish each other. Science looks for what there is, how it got there, and how it relates to the world. Art takes our imagination to explore what might be that we don't yet see and uses creativity as a tool.

Art and science expose the hidden parts of life. "Look what I found!" Someone finds something new and all they want to do is share it with the rest of us. Art and science try to explain what's behind the human experience that's so important to everyone.

A critic looks at art and muses on the meaning in the artist's symbolism. They'll ask, "What do you see? How does it make you feel? What's the artist trying to tell us?" By considering art we see the artist's mind through their creation. Then we see it through our own mind's eye to understand its relevance. Because the message of art is that we have choices.

Science on the other hand describes the world through measurements. It describes the measurable qualities that exist and how they act. And because we're part of the equation it describes how those qualities act on us.

beyond our understanding. If we see ourselves as microcosms of the process then the universe is a system of maturity where questions are reviewed from evolving stages of growth. So through us the universe looks deeper into itself as human history records it. Through love God finds completeness in this limitlessness. So God grows up forever.

To know what's true and dependable—CHALLENGE IT! Prove it. Make it stand up if it's true. Answers are the way to knowing what's real. They show you're on the right track. That's how you build your confidence. Inquiry is the foundation for understanding. And questions and answers are the way you do it.

We all want to know the truth of our style—the style that lets us be ourselves. We want to know who we really are. We want to know we can depend on ourselves. That means having answers. And life's a never-ending knot of questions. And when we solve the riddle, success brings our reward...a new knot!

So we ask, ask, ask! "How do you do that?" "Where do I go?" "What's it cost?" We have to educate ourselves to have what we want. So we evaluate what we've learned, ask more questions, and refine our thoughts into what we use to control the world—our personalities. It's the common thread that joins us to a single design. It doesn't matter if you're a genius or mentally handicapped, everyone questions their experience. Besides our common nature we share a creative mind. And a creative mind means simply that we question things.

ANYWHERE BUT HERE

You might think you need science fiction to take you to some far-off planet. But you really have more than that right here in front of you. Being born put the universe at your doorstep. Here on Earth you have it all. You have oceans and deserts to explore. And you can meet people from the mountains or remote islands. There are a million hidden places and people of all sorts, each with their own way of life. And how they negotiate it is a wonder that'll amaze you.

But if it's space folk you're looking for, beings with antennae and odd features, there's an easier way than going into space. There are Washington lawyers, Iowa farmers, African Pygmies, Arabian princes, Las Vegas entertainers, Europeans, Chinese, Russians, In-dians, and the masses in every culture and each person with a new story to tell. And they're all different. They dress differently. They talk differently. They see the same life you see in a slightly different way. And they do their best to solve life's riddles. And as different as they may seem they're all just like you.

DO IT YOURSELF.

Is being amazed a fair substitute for life's challenges? Doing the work and daring the risks are the rewards in the reality of a challenge. So you have to ask yourself if you have the same opportunity in a real life situation where your mind's racing and your heart's pounding as you do when you're hypnotized by some machine or deferring to some "expert" to solve your problem for you. Isn't it better to master life's stresses than imagine them? Don't be afraid to make mistakes. That's how you learn to accept the pressure of your emotions. The world invites your influence. A career, family, any part of life can be thrilling if you try it.

GO ON.

Every adventure forces you to explore yourself beyond your im-mediate questions about it. They bring up your fears. And you're either overcome by them and emotionally retreat or you favor your interests, take control of your life, and move forward. They test your patience too. So you have to develop your timing. When should you act and when should you wait? It's all part of maturity. And matu-rity protects you while you make your plans for meeting life's new adventures.

GETTING PAST THE ROUGH SPOTS

Part of life's resistance is that sometimes we fail. Inevitably that puts pressure on our sense of right and wrong. We wonder, "Could that failure have been a success if something else was different?" Questioning a failure is the loneliest question in the world. And the answer is always "No." It's God's plan that's paramount. In a moment God can raise you up to the summit of success or drop you down into a pit of disasters—regardless of your best efforts or worst behavior. Life's not just about accomplishments. Life's about engagement. Life's about sincerity. It's about achieving your spiritual clarity.

Every moment's a step on your unending line of experience. Your failures and successes are simply the fuel for the power that energizes your journey. That's all they are. There's always another place to go, another feeling to accept, and another thought to understand. And there's always another step to take. From your first choice as a newborn to the last choice your health allows, you'll move forward with the freedom God gave you. And you'll always want more freedom, more power, and more adventures.

Crises come and go but only the rarest persist. Even the cruelest death passes into the quiet finality of peace. If we weren't somehow conscious of our spirituality would any of us agree to the extreme hardships life demands? It's much easier to volunteer for life's difficulties from an omniscient place in spirit. From that vantage point all possibilities seem reasonable. There the problems make perfect sense. Life's hardships seem a small price to pay for the value of experience that comes with the growth of our souls. But in practice the price can be excessive.

THERE MUST BE AN EASIER WAY.

You might ask yourself why you can't develop spiritually without all the suffering. You'd think that by knowing the truth its value could be better understood just through good directions. This suffering to stimulate conscious awareness seems an excessively harsh burden. The best way for achieving spiritual awareness is probably somewhere in-between. People definitely need less pain and better guidance.

One answer is to have hope. Hope simply means knowing, "You can have it!" When it seems far away, you can be there. When it sounds impossible, it can be done. When it seems too much has to change to give you what you want, hope cuts through the impossibilities with a single word—"Yes." You *can* have it. *It's not impossible.* You can have your soul's fulfillment. So trust it and accept it.

Nothing has more value than your respect for your own thoughts and feelings. There's no complexity, distance, or complication that can tire or confuse you to the point it prevents you from having your dreams come true. While logic says there's a path to your goals, there's a spiritual element to common sense that can lift you beyond the limits of this world.

IT'S ABOUT TIMING.

Your life's a creation in progress. And progress needs time. Think when you worked hard for something for a long time and then as if by magic it all came together in a single day. Life's well represented by the show business adage that it takes twenty years of hard work to be an overnight success. Every morning we find ourselves at the start of a new challenge. And as we resolve our daily conflicts we become a new person. We're better. We're smarter. We've learned from every situation. So we become more confident. Again and again we overcome life's challenges. So, like the trailblazers we are we explore ourselves through every new day.

LiFE'S STAGES

Astronomers talk about the lives of stars. How as they develop they have a unique evolving energy. At their different stages scientists might call them nebulas, red giants, supernovas, or black holes. Human beings are like that too. A life has stages to its journey through time. We begin as infants, grow as toddlers, graduate through school, work, marry, raise families, and then relax into retirement.

And at every stage we have fresh opportunities for learning. Viewing the past through freshly learned insights brings understanding forward through these stages. Understanding the stages realizes the truth about maturity. Maturity is the consolation for enduring life's trials. It's the growing acceptance of your responsibilities. And it's comforting when you finally realize life's a familiar place.

While there's a normal pace for human development, there's also a natural rate unique to each individual. We each have a process and its limits should be respected to understand when we can reasonably expect to do something. Maturity develops as we acquire worldly skills. We learn about costs and benefits. And we learn about value as we develop our priorities. So maturity has the mental focus and emotional agility to respect yourself, respect others, balance your priorities, and make your dreams come true.

Tapping into the Flow

A natural flow of energy surrounds our actions. This is your advantage. You can get a sense of the day's direction beforehand. You can get a feel for what might be successful and what might meet resistance. Whether you think it's "dumb luck" or "To every thing there is a season and a time for every purpose under heaven." sometimes things unexpectedly help us. And sometimes we unexpectedly struggle.

It's like one of those days when you see someone you like but you're totally ignored, an intrusion into the life of a stranger whose attention you crave. Then there are days when everyone you meet—friends and strangers alike—seem infatuated and full of love for you. It's because there's timing to life's energies and it changes every day. So it's important how you put these energy patterns to work for you, because when you manage your life in the energy's direction you'll harmonize your efforts to the world's support.

Pay attention and the patterns reveal themselves. If you can accept the possibility, why not give yourself the benefit of the doubt and explore it? See if it has any value for you. When you make a reasonable effort it's helpful to know there are natural currents in life. Regardless of your efforts, sometimes they'll support you and sometimes they'll resist you. But you can take it into consideration and use it in your daily plans. You can conserve your resources where nature's timing is against you or be more aggressive when your efforts are more in step with nature's process.

The Power in Patience

Often the harshness of our struggle relates to forcing our will against this natural flow of energy. Impatience just adds more resistance.

Trusting the prescribed pace—even if it's a new direction—is always the fastest, easiest, most direct, and most rewarding path to your goals. Patience means trusting that the direction of life's energies is in your best interests.

Faith sees the patterns in life. It reveals more than just what's on the surface of our minds. It acknowledges that some things happen for no other reason than these energies support them. Life's energies are God's directions. So, faith in God determines our time to dream, our time to plan, and the right time to act. Believing that you have to have it all, all the time, lacks confidence in life. Life's demands are constant;

FIND A PASSION

Human beings crave newness but it's not out of boredom. Whatever we find we use to explore our lives. And while we don't always attach such lofty ideals to our reasoning, just the same, that's exactly what we do.

So it's a blessing to have a hobby or be passionate about anything. It's a gift to find something that inspires you. A passion can suspend time for you. It can elevate you beyond the confusion of this demanding world so only the joy of your involvement remains. It's something you love doing so much that you'd do it even if you didn't get paid for it. And when you really do it, beyond the magazines and small talk, you'll discover that there's real pleasure in life's accomplishments. Whether it's rollerblading, politics, or playing in a band, finding a passion is the way to discover your joy in life. Then you'll be a true explorer.

So find out what you like and invest your soul in it. Design and build it. When you honor your passions with action it guarantees you revelations. And you'll achieve a personal harmony that transcends any balance you've created before. That harmony reflects on everyone. And you'll be a role model to those who also seek the truth you've found.

sometimes explosive, sometimes oppressive, and sometimes dismissive. Life's support is equally constant; sometimes leading, sometimes waiting, and sometimes hiding. But the subtleties reveal its nature. And when you sense it you can move in harmony with it.

That's what happens when powerful events shock us back to consciousness. Like a car accident or unexpected promotion, jolts of experience should be understood as guiding spirits meant to trigger a conscious change in our lives. Communications from spirit are reflected in the details of our lives. They represent important things we should pay attention to. Life won't take anything from you that you can't live without. Or ever give you more than you can handle. But critical lessons demand your attention and are often indicated by sudden or unusual events.

THE "HOLY GRAIL"

Life exists for opportunities, not limits. Life's limits are its opportunities. Life will either coax you or shove you in the right direction. But, right for what? Only you and God know for sure. Others who've been through similar situations can help with evaluation but something priceless is gained through your experience. You move into an experience, through it, and beyond it. And you become a new person. You're unavoidably changed by it. You explored the experience and learned what it taught you.

We grow through our successes as much as we grow through our failures. We love ourselves completely when we respect every experience. Any success can have its painful parts. And any problem can be blessed with love. Nothing is separate from everything else. That's what makes life so interesting. It's a challenge to make it all work together. But to build anything you first have to build yourself into someone you can trust. There you'll find harmony with your partner...LIFE! That's the meaning of success.

It's exciting to be a human being, a living soul. Because we're all treasure hunters looking for that Holy Grail with our name on it. It's our purpose and protection. And with patience and imagination it's the path we take that invigorates God's adventure.

Think About It — Chapter 6

Thought #1: *When we move through an experience with an appreciation for its value everything about it is worthwhile.*

Thought #2: *We're always asking ourselves, "Where do I fit in?" "What do I want?" "What should I do?" Questioning things is what it means to be alive—self-examination and the constant search for answers.*

Thought #3: *Fashionable ideas limit self-expression. Exploration is about reaching out from your safe place on life's carousel and taking a risk.*

Thought #4: *A natural flow of energy surrounds our actions. That gives you an advantage. You can get a sense of the day's direction beforehand and have an idea what might be successful and what might meet resistance.*

Thought #5: *We may dismay in the endless frustrations at the heart of this adventure. But it's our glory when we see them as ways to explore ourselves.* **Thanks to God.**

EASY ORDER FORM

To order _Spiriting Around: A Modern Guide to Finding Yourself_

Fax Orders to: (954) 435-8662 _Just Fill In And Fax This Form_

Telephone Orders to: Dial Toll Free 1-87 SKY HIGH 0 (zero)

Email Orders to: easyorder@spiritingaround.com

Mail Orders to: Mooring Field Books, 9369 Sheridan St., #555 Cooper City, FL 33024 USA

I would like to order (Qty) _____ book(s) @ $14.95 each plus shipping & handling of $5.95 each for delivery addresses in the continental U.S. Please add 6% sales tax for orders shipped to Florida.

Please send my book(s) to:

Name: _____

Address: _____

City: _____ State: _____ Zip Code: _____

Telephone: (_____) _____

Email: _____

Payment via: 1) ☐ Check/Money Order enclosed $ _____
                   2) ☐ Credit Card

Credit Card Type: ☐ Visa ☐ MasterCard ☐ American Express ☐ Discover

Card Number: _____

Signature: _____ Exp. Date: _____ / _____

All books are shipped as ground packages
United States Postal Service unless otherwise requested.

☐ FedEx_____ ☐ UPS_____

☐ Other_____

Type of Service: _____ Date: ____/____/____
(At standard published rates)

If you're not completely satisfied please return your order for a full refund.

Thank you for ordering _Spiriting Around_.

MOORING FIELD BOOKS Inc.

* Please call for bulk ordering information.